LEARN IN   15 MINUTES

calligraphy

METRO BOOKS
New York

An Imprint of Sterling Publishing Co., Inc.
1166 Avenue of the Americas
New York, NY 10036

© 2017 Quarto Publishing Plc.

ISBN 978-1-4351-6655-4

For information about custom editions, special sales, and premium
and corporate purchases, please contact Sterling Special Sales at
800-805-5489 or specialsales@sterlingpublishing.com.

Manufactured in China

2 4 6 8 10 9 7 5 3 1

www.sterlingpublishing.com

Produced by Rotovision, an imprint of the Quarto Group
Publisher: Mark Searle
Editorial Director: Isheeta Mustafi
Commissioning Editor: Emily Angus
Junior Editor: Abbie Sharman
Project Manager: Lindsay Kaubi
Page Design: J C Lanaway
Cover Concept and Design: Karen Hood

LEARN IN 15 MINUTES

calligraphy

15 EXERCISES • 15 TECHNIQUES • 15 VARIATIONS

WILLIAM PATERSON

METRO BOOKS
New York

Contents

Introduction

I had a calligraphy set when I was a child, but I began learning calligraphy in earnest when I was 18 and I have since developed, adapted, and practiced my skills to reach the point where I was able to create this book and pass on some of my experience of calligraphy and hand lettering. I hope you'll enjoy learning the many skills and styles that are featured throughout the pages. I love the free-flowing look of calligraphy and the way it can appear so effortless, but strangely, despite the sense of freedom that calligraphy can give, it's important to remember that the guidelines that are used in calligraphy and lettering are essential in making your work look good!

This book is designed to allow you to learn the basics, and then to move into more advanced styles and variations—you might even find your signature style on the way! It is organized into three sections:

Calligraphy Exercises—This is written lettering and involves applying varying degrees of pressure to a pen to create lettering all in a single stroke. In this section you'll learn about copperplate, italics, and using brush pens, among many other things.

Lettering Techniques—This section focuses on drawing letters rather than writing them. In this section you will discover different styles, such as sans serif, signature style, and vintage brush script.

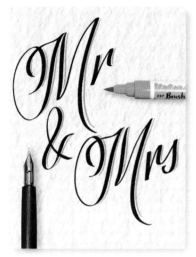

Within each of the three sections there are 15 bite-sized lessons that break down the skills needed for successful calligraphy. If you see the nib symbol, this means that the lesson's steps continue onto the next page. Between each exercise are blank or lined pages where you can try out the technique described on the preceding pages. For some tutorials you can connect the dots on these pages to create extra lines as needed (for example, if you need a narrow space between the ascender and cap height line).

Calligraphy and lettering can be difficult if you're just starting out, but I encourage you to stick with it and keep practicing as it will pay off in the end! Remember the importance of weighting and guidelines and equip yourself with good quality pens, pencils, and paper. But most of all, enjoy it! Calligraphy has brought me so much joy over the years and I'm glad I stuck it out!

Variations and Extras—These are the decorative flourishes and effects that can be added to your calligraphy and lettering. Here you will learn how to devise successful lettering compositions, add shadows to your lettering, and use effects such as stippling and watercolor.

William Paterson

15 Calligraphy Exercises

Hard Pointed Brush Pen

The key to the pointed brush pen technique is remembering to apply heavy pressure as you move your hand towards you, and light pressure when it is traveling away.

1. If you are using your own paper, start by drawing straight horizontal guides for the cap height, baseline, median, and descender height.

2. Hold your pen at a 45-degree angle and, applying heavy pressure, move your pen down toward the baseline. Make sure the pressure you are applying remains constant.

3. Repeat step 2 in reverse but only apply very light pressure and begin at the baseline, moving your pen upward.

4. Maintaining a 45-degree angle, start at the top of the x-height and move your pen downward applying heavy pressure until you reach the baseline. Complete the stroke by moving the pen upward and applying light pressure from the baseline to the middle of the x-height.

5. Start at the baseline, applying light pressure, travel toward the top of the x-height before turning back on yourself, applying heavier pressure, and returning to the baseline.

6. Repeat steps 2 through to 5 to complete the form in its entirety.

7. Image 7 demonstrates why this is a "hard brush" script. Nearly all of the strokes are fast and abrupt. Practice writing the word "minimum" to gain consistency in your strokes.

8. Apply heavy pressure as you start at the x-height and travel toward the baseline, before curving slightly as you arch back toward the x-height to complete the "o."

9. Repeat step 4 but start from the cap height.

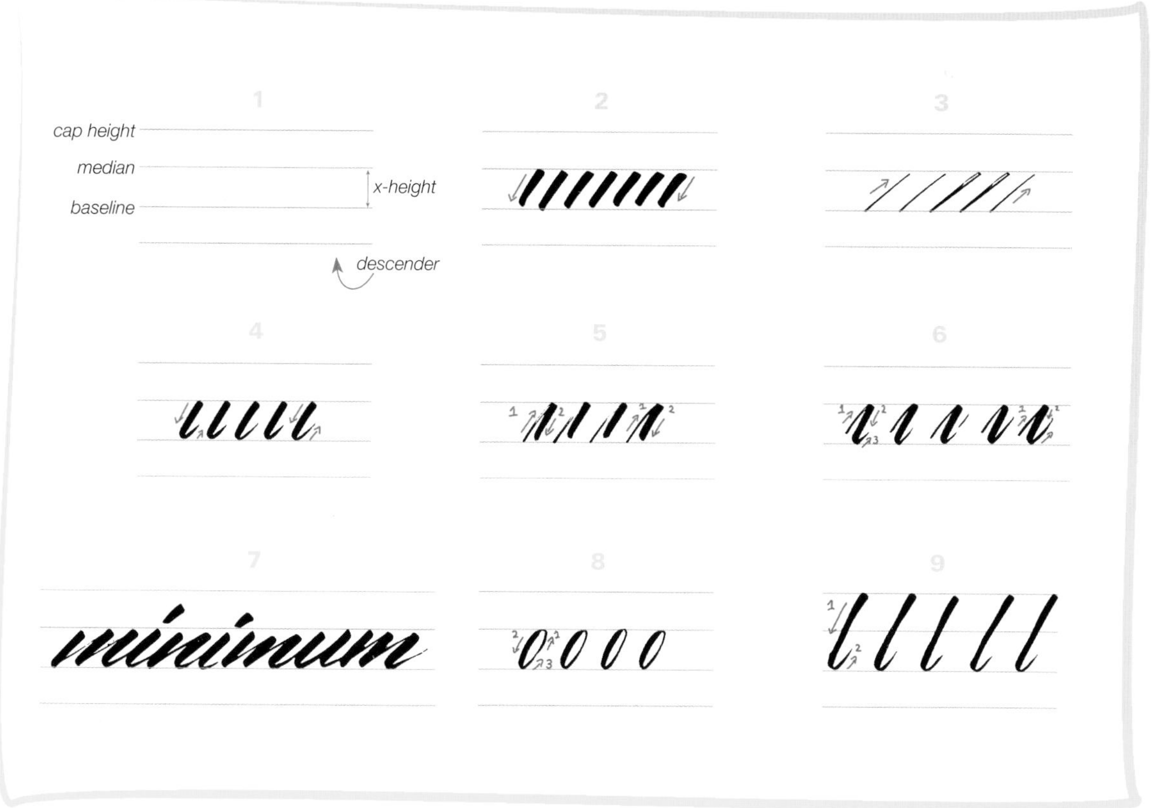

cap height

median

baseline

x-height

descender

minimum

PRACTICE YOUR EXERCISES HERE

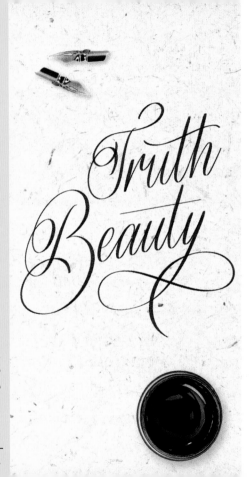

Copperplate

To perfect your copperplating, practice exercises that will improve your angling, strokes, and strokes which have movement. Completing two lines of each exercise before moving on to the next will help you develop.

1. On the following page, draw a line to connect the first set of dots and use this line as your ascender. Repeat this step for the rest of the guides as needed. Add lines at a 45-degree angle, then turn your paper so it is vertical and, using a Nikko G Nib with an oblique pen holder, align your nib with the 45-degree lines. Create strokes from the baseline to the ascender line, using light pressure.

2. Now, make the same stroke but move the pen downward from the ascender to the baseline and apply heavier pressure.

3. This stroke is the same as step 2 but with a curve to the right. Remember to reduce the pressure before starting to curve.

4. Now complete a shorter version of the stroke in step 3. Start at the top of the x-height and add a short, light upstroke, finishing at half of the x-height.

5. Repeat step 4 but upside-down. Start with a light upstroke that curves into a heavy downstroke. This is a standard starting stroke for arching letters, such as "n," "m," "p," "v," and "w." Begin the light upstroke on the baseline.

6. Join together steps 4 and 5 so that you have a light upstroke, heavy downstroke, and light upstroke again.

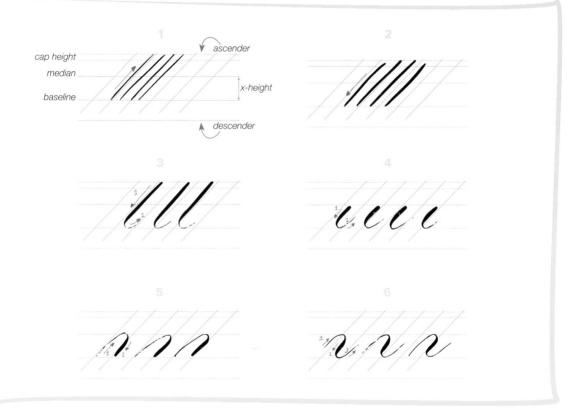

7. Starting on the right side about a quarter from the top, create a light upstroke counterclockwise and draw the "o" in a single stroke, getting thicker as you go around to the left, and then a light upstroke to meet on the right.

8. Complete a standard lead-in stroke applying light pressure and a slight curve. This is used to start the letters "t," "j," "u," "l," "f," "h," "k," "s," and "e."

9. Practice writing the word "million."

PRACTICE YOUR EXERCISES HERE

Monoline Script

Monoline Script is a vintage favorite on Instagram. Monoline is exactly what the name suggests; all the letters have a consistent weight. This means you can be really creative with flourishes and composition. A Pentel Paint Marker is ideal for this style.

1. If using your own paper, start by drawing straight horizontal guides for the cap height, baseline, median, and descender height. You could also draw vertical guidelines at a 65-degree angle if you're not confident.

2. Using a marker pen, start by drawing straight lines from the median line to the baseline. Keep practicing until all the lines you draw are consistent. The angle of the lines should be around 65 degrees.

3. Starting from the median line, draw down to the baseline. Before you hit the baseline, curve the line to create the connector. Achieving a consistent result is difficult, so make sure you keep practicing until you're confident.

4. Repeat the exercise in step 3 in reverse and, instead of starting from the median guideline, start from the center of the x-height.

cap height

median

baseline

x-height

descender

1

2

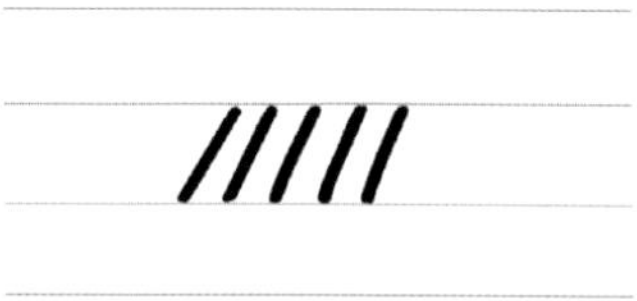

3

4

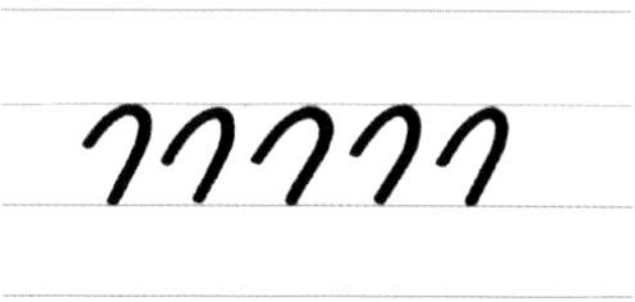

5. Now combine the exercises in steps 3 and 4. The trick is to have the bowl of each letter as round as possible. You should be able to draw a perfect circle inside the bowl.

6. Starting from the middle of the x-height, draw ovals. This can be difficult but make sure you keep practicing.

7. If you want to write a specific word, try drawing the skeleton lightly in pencil first. This gives you a guideline to go by when using the pen.

8. The finished lettering should look as uniform and consistent as in image 8.

PRACTICE YOUR EXERCISES HERE

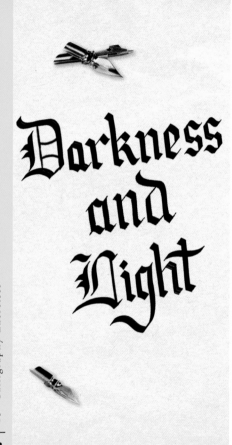

Gothic Calligraphy

Gothic is a really versatile calligraphy style; there are many different variations with which you can experiment. One of the most attractive aspects of Gothic calligraphy is the boldness and the consistency in all the letterforms. All Gothic letterforms hold to a pattern, which you'll learn in the exercises below.

1. Join the first set of dots on the practice pages and use this as your ascender line. Repeat this step for the rest of the guides. Use a Pilot Parallel pen and make sure the flat nib is at a 45-degree angle. This is important in order to create balance and consistency through all the letters. Make a series of vertical downstrokes as shown in image 1.

2. Holding your pen at the same angle, create diagonal downstrokes, this will give you a thick line. Try to make the strokes look the same.

3. Hold your pen at the same angle and repeat step 2, but this time travel from the median height to the baseline. If this is done correctly, you should get very thin lines.

4. Now create a series of diamonds. Keep these as consistent as possible.

5. Stating from the median height create a diamond, then repeat step 1. Now create another diamond at the baseline. This formation is the basis for nearly all the lowercase Gothic letterforms.

6. Repeat the exercise in step 5 but this time complete all the steps in one continuous stroke.

7. Image 7 shows a word drawn in the Gothic alphabet.

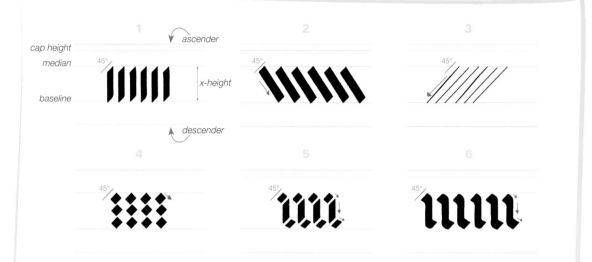

cap height
median
baseline
ascender
x-height
descender

1 45°
2 45°
3 45°
4 45°
5 45°
6 45°

7

gothic

23

PRACTICE YOUR EXERCISES HERE

Ruling Pen Calligraphy

The ruling pen was invented to draw precise lines and in the past was used mainly by engineers and draftsmen. Today ruling pens are often used by calligraphers because of the contrast in weight that can be achieved. Here, you'll learn some pen strokes that will familiarize you with ruling pens.

1. Start by drawing downstrokes, working from thin to thick. Create thin strokes by holding the pen vertically and then gradually flatten the angle of the pen for the thickest stroke.

2. Using the flat side of the ruling pen, draw downstrokes and end them with a flick.

3. This time, start from the baseline and, using the tip of the pen, make a light diagonal upstroke, then pull into a downstroke finishing at the baseline.

4. Hold your pen flat to the paper so that you get the thickest stroke, and pull down to create an arch to the baseline. Then, using the tip of the pen, flick up to the median height to create an "o."

5. Repeat the exercise in step 3, but then pull to create a thick line ending with a slight flick that is horizontal to the baseline.

6. This is a descender stoke. Start as you did for step 2, but carry on past the baseline to the descender height, finishing by easing the pressure off the pen and creating a flick to the left.

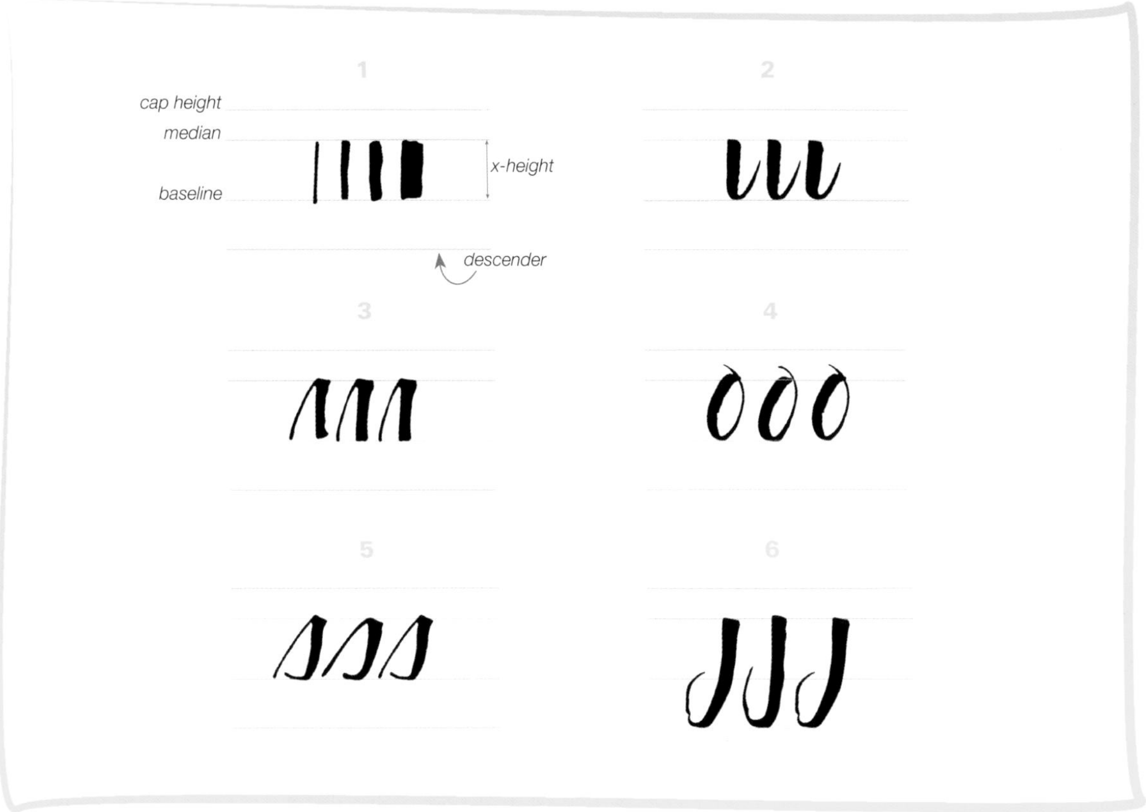

cap height

median

baseline

x-height

1

2

descender

3

4

5

6

PRACTICE YOUR EXERCISES HERE

Smooth Pointed Brush Pen

You can produce a smoother looking pointed brush form by repeating what you learned on pages 10–11; however, the application or removal of pressure from the nib is less abrupt. These exercises will help you to master this.

1. If you are using your own paper, start by drawing straight horizontal guides for the cap height, baseline, median, and descender height. Then, starting at the median and positioning your pen at a 45-degree angle, apply heavy pressure as you head toward the baseline.

2. Applying lighter pressure and beginning at the baseline, repeat step 1 in reverse.

3. Repeat step 1 but, as you approach the baseline, begin to curve upward, gradually applying less pressure as you travel toward the median.

4. Starting at the baseline repeat step 2 but curve the line at the the median, gradually applying more pressure, as you did in step 3, and return to the baseline.

5. Combine steps 1 to 4 to complete the form in its entirety, as shown opposite.

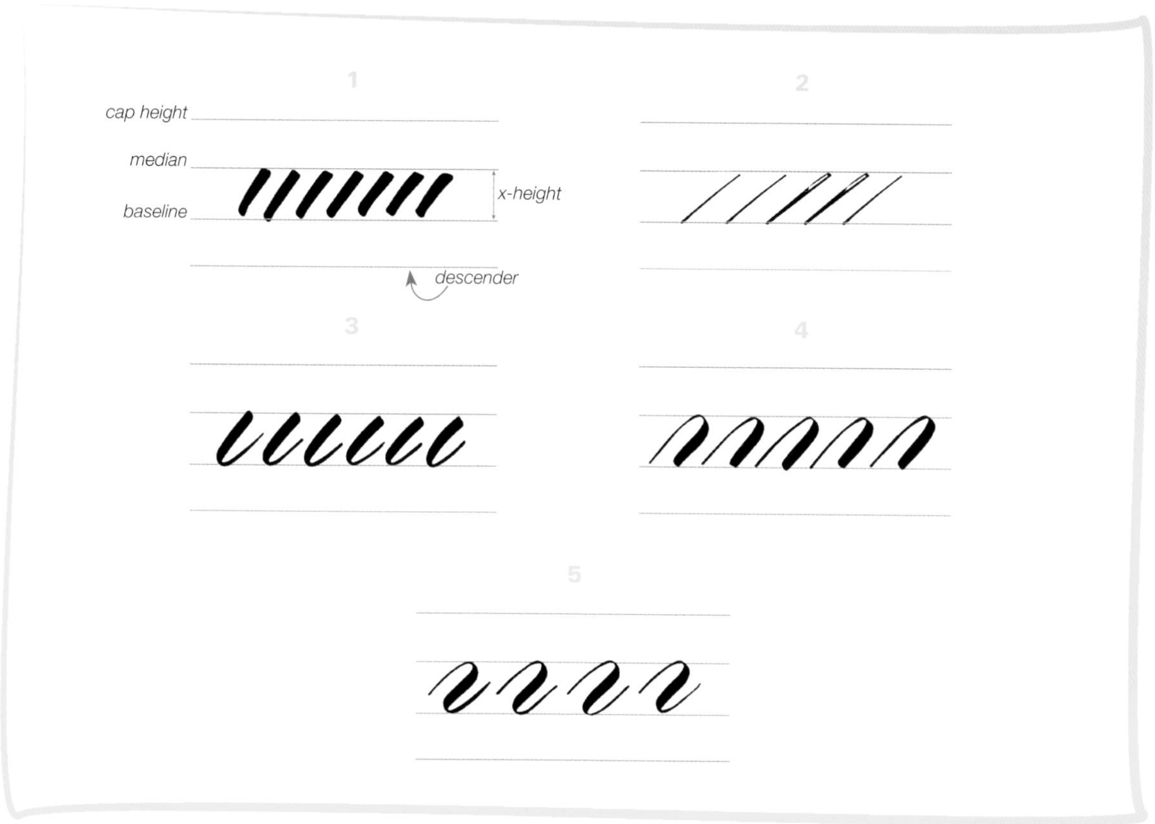
1
cap height
median
baseline
x-height
descender
2
3
4
5

6. Start at the median and apply heavy pressure as you travel toward the baseline. As you curve at the baseline, gradually take off the pressure and arch back toward the median to complete the "o."

7. Repeat the exercise in step 6 but when you have finished your stroke add a connector to the right of the "o."

8. Practice writing the word "Aluminum" or "minimum." This exercise will help you to gain consistency when creating these letterforms.

PRACTICE YOUR EXERCISES HERE

Modern Brush Script

The main difference between the old school and modern brush calligraphy is the way in which the letterforms are created. Follow the images and complete the exercises below carefully, following the corresponding red numbers and arrows to learn how to create modern-style brush script. Use an Ecoline Brush pen for this style.

1. For this exercise your ascender line needs to be closer to your cap height, so use the dots provided on the practice page to lower the line. Hold your Ecoline Brush Pen at 0 degrees, so that the brush tip is pointing to the left. This is important so that you can get a consistent line. Applying pressure, create three to six lines, working from the median to the baseline.

2. Now do the opposite to step 1. Starting from the baseline, while holding your pen at the same angle, create three to six vertical lines applying light pressure.

3. Repeat step 1, but while traveling to the baseline create a curve and repeat step 2.

4. Repeat step 3 but this time start from the middle of the x-height. Travel upward and curve and then draw a straight line to the baseline.

5. Join the exercises in steps 3 and 4 together.

6. To create an "o," start from the middle of the x-height, travel upwards, and repeat step 1 with a slight curve. Then repeat step 3.

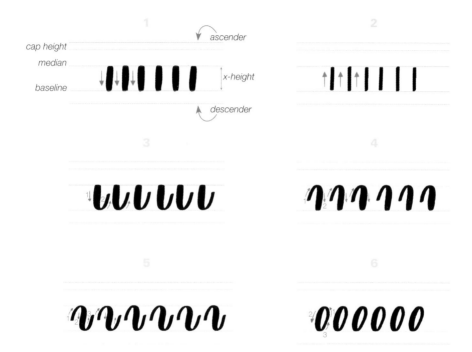

7. Repeat step 3 but this time start from the ascender height.

8. Now create part of the letterform found in the letters "b" and "p." Repeat exercise 4 but, this time, instead of creating a straight line create a curved line to the baseline.

9. Image 9 shows how brush script works in a word. Notice how inaccurate it can be; modern brush calligraphy doesn't have to be perfect, in fact, the imperfections of the letterforms are desirable.

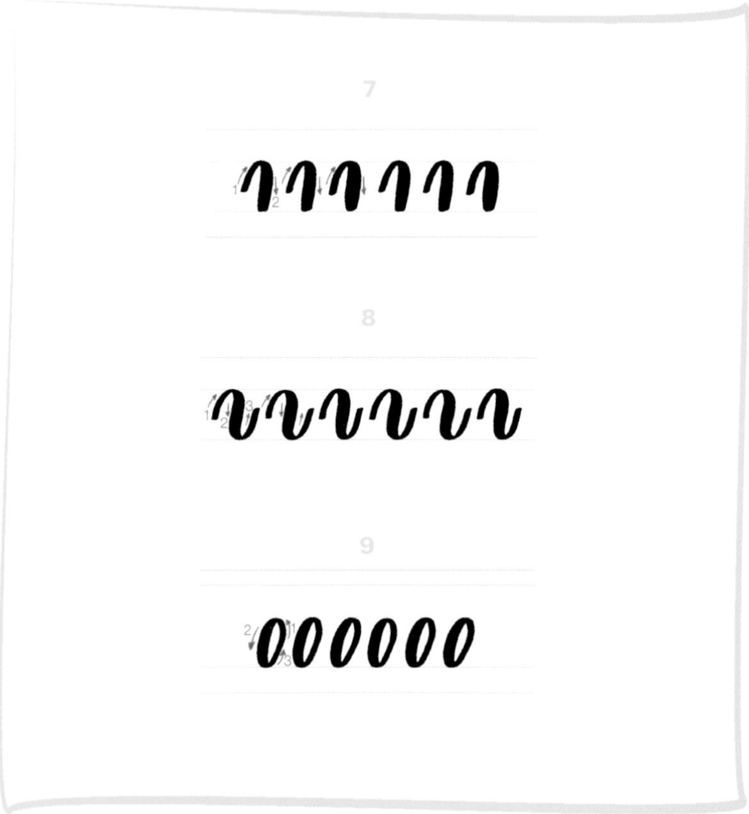

7

8

9

PRACTICE YOUR EXERCISES HERE

Watercolor Calligraphy

Calligraphy is an art form that is becoming ever more popular. This means that people are experimenting with different tools and being more creative in the way in which calligraphy is made; watercolor calligraphy is good example of a newer, more creative use of tools. The exercises below will teach you how to apply your skills when using a new tool.

1. Watercolor lettering is similar to normal brush lettering. The only differences are the ink and the pen. To start, use a round brush—preferably sable—and normal watercolor paint.

2. Mix your watercolor paint with water and, working on watercolor paper, begin to use the watercolor brush to letter out your word. The great thing about watercolor calligraphy is that it can be rough, it doesn't need to be formal. Keep in mind that, depending on the paper and how much water/ paint you use, you may need to tape your paper down to avoid warping.

PRACTICE YOUR EXERCISES HERE

Casual Brush Script

Casual script is used by sign painters to create quick "one stroke" lettering for shop signage. It gives a really bold and playful look to lettering compositions. The brushes used for this are different to brush pens, but you can still achieve the effect by using Ecoline Brush Pens.

1. If you are using your own paper, use straight horizontal guides for the cap height, baseline, median, and descender height. On the practice pages, join the first set of dots for each set of guides and use the new line as your ascender guide. Join the fourth set of dots to narrow the distance from the baseline to your descender line. Start by applying pressure and making a series of thick lines at an angle of 60 degrees between the cap height and baseline.

2. Casual script is different to other lettering because the brush pen needs to physically change direction to produce the desired thickness and effect. Create a series of horizontal lines on the baseline, half as thick as the vertical lines in step 1.

3. As you can see in image 3, the letter "A" is made up of two down strokes and one side stroke. It's worth keeping in mind that the casual script alphabet is primarily made up of thick down strokes! Try recreating the "A" shown in image 3.

4. Now create a half circle; this is half a capital "O." Start by applying pressure at the cap height and travel down to the baseline with an arch to the left.

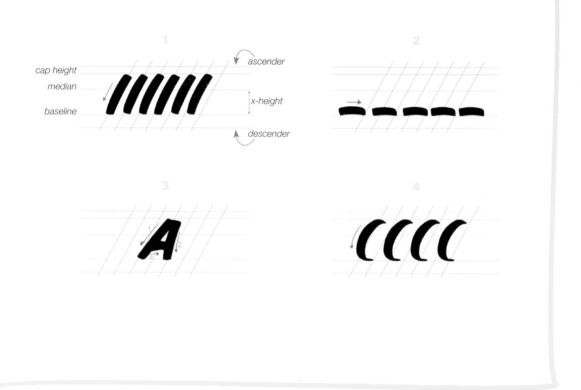

5. Now create the second half of the "O" by repeating step 4 but working to the right. Once you've successfully created a consistent shape doing this, try creating the whole "O" by joining steps 4 and 5 together.

6. Repeat step 2 but this time start and finish at the cap height.

7. As you can see, casual script is informal and playful. When writing in casual script, always keep in mind that the letterforms are very close to each other; increasing the kerning (spacing between each letterform) will make the word appear unbalanced.

PRACTICE YOUR EXERCISES HERE

Italic Calligraphy

Italic calligraphy is a very elegant form of writing. A broad pen is used to achieve the differences in weight; a Parallel Pilot Pen or a Brause 3mm nib are ideal for this. Follow the steps below to perfect this style of calligraphy.

1. Establish a 45-degree angle on paper by creating a series of downstrokes. The pen angle for italic is mainly 45 degrees, so make sure to default to that angle.

2. This next exercise is to make sure that your pen angle is at 45 degrees. If you maintain the angle correctly, then you should achieve a series of thick and thin lines.

3. Repeat the exercise in step 1, but this time add an upstroke after the downstrokes. This forms the basis of the letters "n" and "m."

4. This time create an "o." Start with a downstroke and a thin upstroke as in step 3, then join both strokes with a small horizontal stroke.

5. Now try writing the word "minimum." Writing this word gives you an accurate representation of how consistent each stroke is. Keep practicing these exercises to gain more control and consistency.

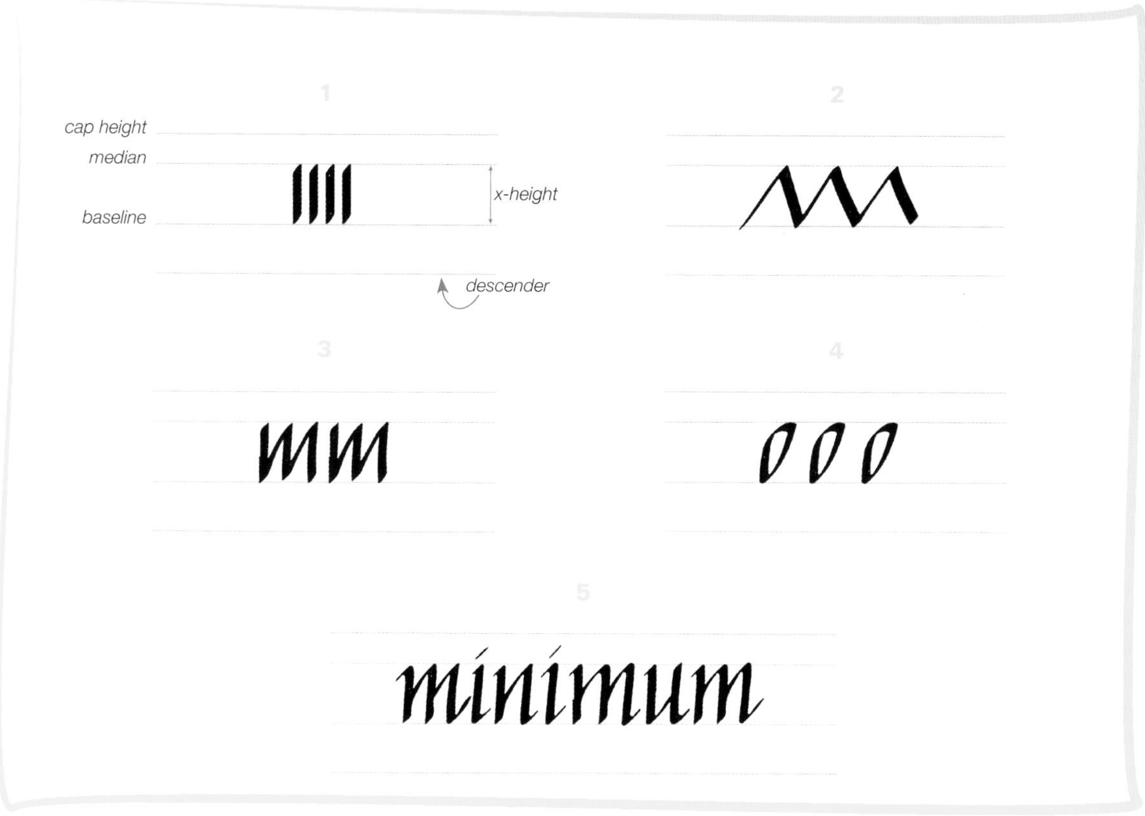
1
cap height
median
baseline
x-height
descender
2
3
4
5
minimum

PRACTICE YOUR EXERCISES HERE

Crayola Calligraphy

Calligraphy has evolved in recent years. As more people take up calligraphy, more experimentation with different tools is taking place. The Crayola marker is inexpensive but works better than some professional brush pens!

1. Start by using the edge of the Crayola marker to create a thick line from the median to the baseline.

2. Repeat step 1, but this time use the tip of the Crayola marker to create a thin line. You should clearly see the difference between the weight of the thick and thin lines.

3. Repeat step 1 and follow it with step 2 when you hit the baseline. Keep repeating this exercise until your strokes are as consistent as possible.

4. Starting from just below the median, travel 45-degrees upward, then repeat step 1 followed by step 2.

5. Join the strokes in steps 4 and 3 together to create a lowercase "a."

6. This time repeat step 3, but start from the cap height. Keep in mind that Crayola calligraphy can be tricky at first, but try not to be slow when creating the letterforms; it should be done at a quick pace.

7. Image 7 shows how the Crayola marker works as a brush pen.

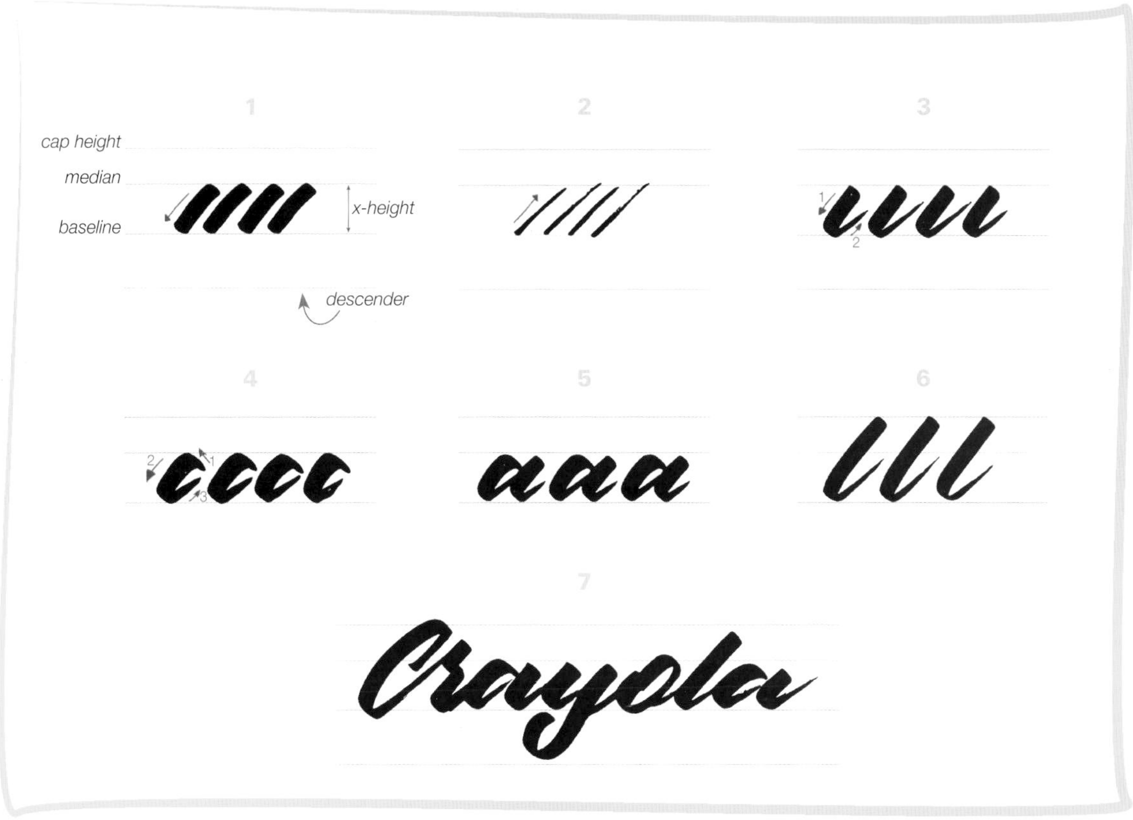
1
2
3
cap height
median
baseline
x-height
descender
4
5
6
7
Crayola

PRACTICE YOUR EXERCISES HERE

Business Script

Business script is a type of formal writing that is traditionally written with a fountain pen. It's a way of writing elegantly and quickly without getting hand cramps. Learn how to create business script by following the exercises below.

1. This may be easier using writing paper or dot-grid paper. On the following page, join the third set of dots for each set of guides. Use the new line as your baseline. Depending on your desired look, you can use a fountain pen or a rollerball pen; avoid biro as it won't work with the flow of the type.

2. First, create a letter "i." You need your arm to be parallel to the paper, so get into a comfortable position and move the paper if needed. Starting from the baseline, draw a connector line and then pull down toward your body and create another connector line.

3. Now draw the "o." The trick is to keep doing this consistently on the same line without taking your pen off the paper. Take care not to strain your arm when doing this!

4. Now draw the "a." The "a" is just the same as the "o," but with an "i" resting against it.

5. Make sure to give your letters plenty of room; there should be a letter length between each letter so that it's legible.

6. To draw an "n" all you have to do is draw an "i" with a zigzag following it. This one can be hard to perfect as it can confuse your muscle memory.

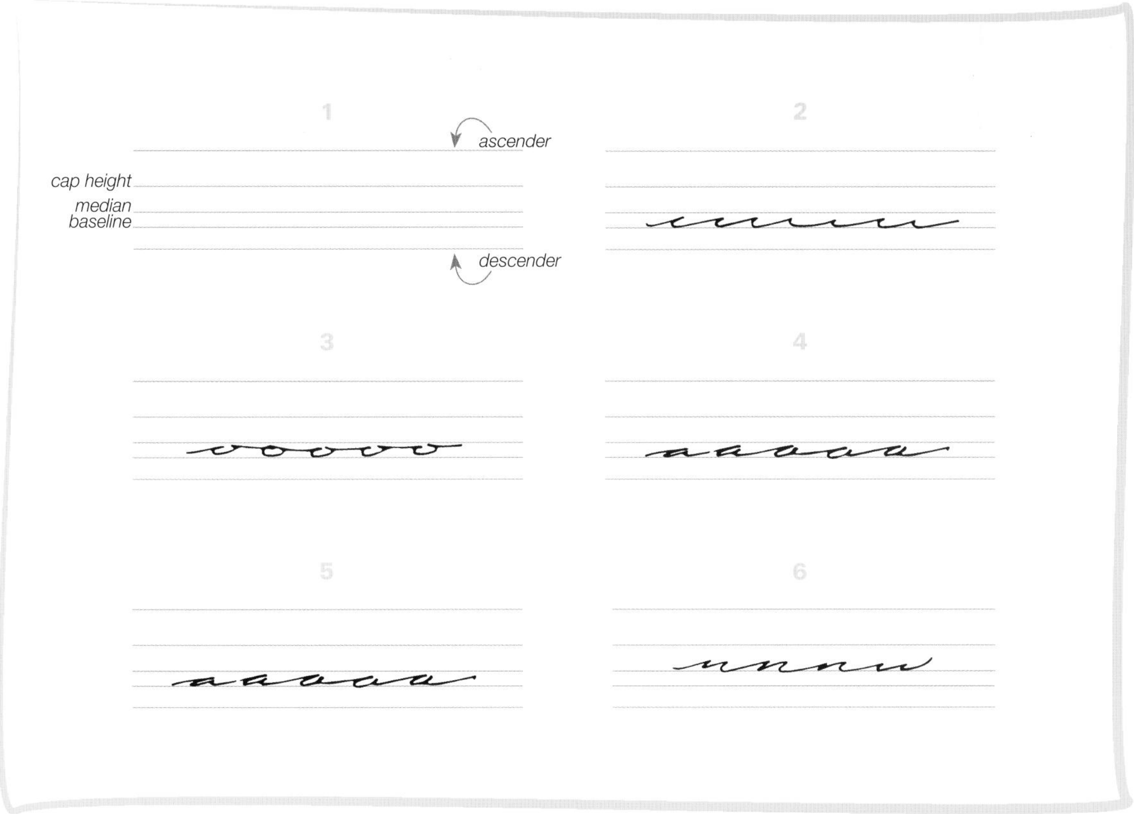

1

cap height
median
baseline

ascender

descender

2

ururu

3

ooooo

4

aaaaa

5

aaaaa

6

nnnnu

7. The "m" is just the same as the "n" but with an extra zigzag.

8. Once you've practiced the exercises try writing the word "mine"; this is a great word to practice with because it will show your ability to remain consistent.

9. Image 9 shows how this style should look to the reader.

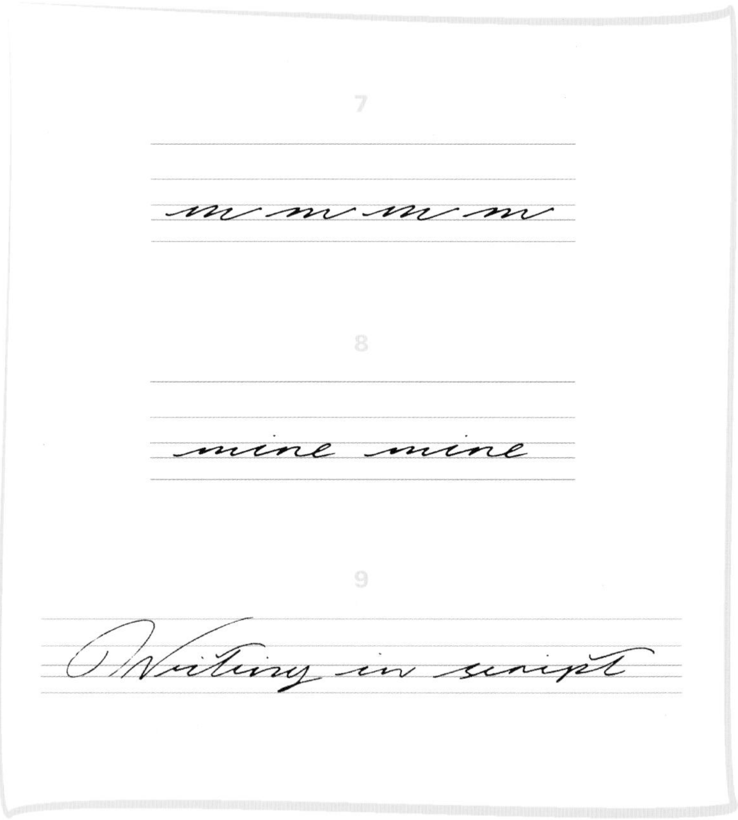

PRACTICE YOUR EXERCISES HERE

Foundational

Foundational is one of the best scripts for learning the basics of minuscules (lower-case letters) within broad-pen calligraphy. Foundational is sometimes called "minimalist" because its simplicity and the spacing between each letter gives it an elegant appearance. Use a Pilot Parallel Pen for this style.

1. Start by creating a series of vertical downstrokes with your broad pen (Pilot Parallel Pen) at a 30-degree angle. It's important to keep your pen angle at 30 degrees when writing in foundational. You should also keep your lines as consistent as possible.

2. To create the first part of the "o," start from the median and create a half circle that stretches down to the baseline.

3. Repeat the stroke in exercise 2 but this time reverse it to complete the "o."

4. Add some subtle arcs to the top and bottom of the downstroke. These are the serifs.

5. Repeat the exercise in step 4, then connect your new downstrokes to the prior downstroke. Repeat this until you get a pattern as seen in image 5. Make sure to give yourself lots of room in-between each stroke.

6. Repeat the strokes in exercise 5 but this time reverse them.

7. Now that you've practiced the system for foundational, try writing "onion." Your letters should look flowing and consistent.

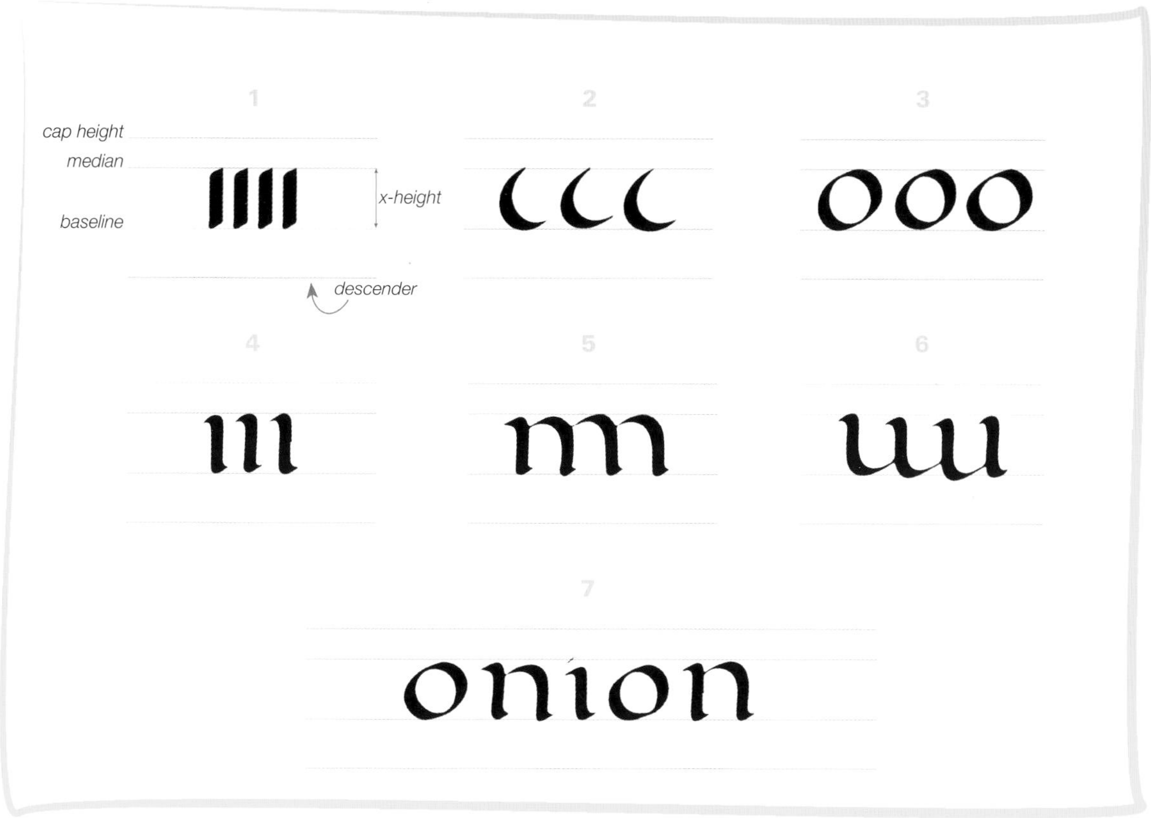

cap height

median

baseline

x-height

descender

1

2

3

4

5

6

7

onion

Neuland

Neuland is a very different looking type of calligraphy. Some consider it to be a little simpler, but it can work extremely well within a calligraphy composition. Use a Pilot Parallel pen or a broad-nib pen to achieve the Neuland style.

1. Holding the pen at 0 degrees, create a series of simple vertical downstrokes.

2. Turn the pen to 90 degrees and, using the thickest part of the pen, draw a horizontal line along the top of the cap height, repeating the same line underneath until you reach the baseline.

3. Turn the pen to 30 degrees and pull a diagonal line downward from left to right.

4. Repeat the exercise in step 3 but in reverse.

5. Holding the pen at 0 degrees, draw a half-circle shape, aligning top to bottom as best you can. This may take some practice to get it right!

6. Repeat the exercise in step 5 but in reverse. This is will be the other half of the "o."

7. Holding the pen at 0 degrees, draw a vertical downstroke, then taper into a slight curve at the baseline.

8. Repeat the exercise in step 7 but in reverse.

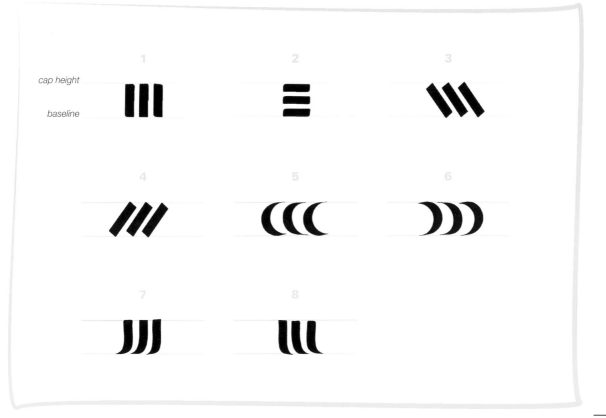

cap height

baseline

9. Holding the pen at 90 degrees, draw a convex horizontal arc. Repeat the arc in the opposite direction while maintaining the consistency.

10. Holding the pen at 0 degrees, draw a curve and swing back into a counter-curve. This is the foundational stroke for the "S." Try to keep the top and bottom consistent with each other.

11. Draw an "o" in four strokes starting with step 5, add exercise 9, and join up with exercise 6.

PRACTICE YOUR EXERCISES HERE

Roman

The Roman alphabet is one of the most versatile and legible typefaces in use. It's popular for hand lettering because of the possibilities for embellishing the type. These exercises will teach you the correct hand movements and pen angles for Roman lettering. Use a Pilot Parallel Pen or a broad-nib pen for these exercises.

1. Holding the pen at a 30-degree angle, draw a series of downstrokes from the cap height to the baseline. Keep the angle and spacing of the lines as consistent as possible.

2. Holding the pen at a 20-degree angle, create a column of horizontal lines starting at the cap height and ending at the baseline.

3. Holding the pen at a 45-degree angle, create a series of diagonal side strokes from the cap height to the baseline. If you're holding your pen correctly these should be thin lines.

4. Repeat the exercise in step 3, holding your pen at the same 45-degree angle but this time pull the downstroke to your right. This should create a series of thick downstrokes.

5. Holding the pen at a 30-degree angle, draw a half circle, similar to a crescent.

6. Repeat the exercise in step 5, but in the opposite direction.

7. Repeat the exercises in steps 5 and 6, but this time combine them to form an "o."

8. Holding the pen at a 30-degree angle, create an S-curve starting from the cap height and ending at the baseline.

9. Practice writing the word "ROMAN."

ROMAN

PRACTICE YOUR EXERCISES HERE

Gallery

RIGHT Serif flourishes and a swash add elegance and help to balance this typeface layout.

Non-letter organic decorative
elements, monoline calligraphy, and
a circular composition make this
composition feel fun and outdoorsy.

LEFT Circular arch shapes guide the
formal serif type at the top; a drawn
element forms the center of the design;
and cursive script at the bottom
balances the composition.

15 Lettering Techniques

Vintage Brush Script

Brush pens are great for creating the "brush calligraphy look"; however, this can be limiting as there's only so much you can do with a brush pen. In this tutorial you will learn the absolute basics for hand lettering brush script with a pencil.

1. If you are using your own paper, lightly draw two lines using the top and bottom edges of your ruler. These indicate the baseline and the ascender height. Now use the ruler to draw out the descender height and median. On the practice pages, connect the fourth set of dots for each set of guides. The new line will become your descender guide.

2. Next, draw several 65-degree angled lines—you could use a ruler for this if you like. It's not essential to have a perfect 65-degree angle, but it is important that the lines you draw are consistent.

3. Start drawing the skeleton of the lettering. Make sure the angle of the vertical lines of your lettering adheres to the 65-degree angle. This is the foundation of your lettering.

4. Now start to lightly add weight to the skeleton. The distribution of the weight should mimic exactly how a brush would distribute the weight. For a reminder of this, read "Smooth Pointed Brush Pen" on pages 30–32.

5. You should now have a rough idea of what the brush lettering looks like. You may notice that it doesn't look "clean." This is perfectly normal. Using tracing paper or a light box, trace your lettering with a sharp pencil, then fill in your letterforms with a fine-liner, such as a Micron 01.

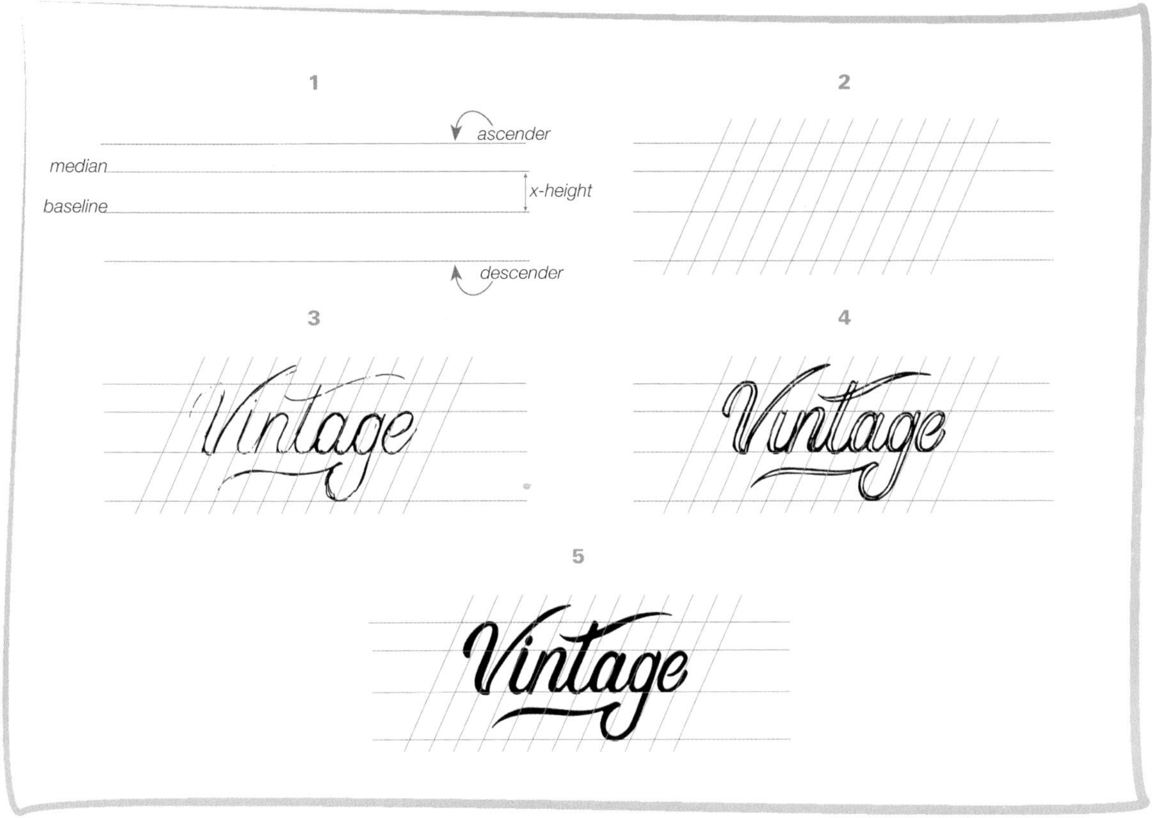

1

ascender

median

baseline

x-height

descender

2

3

Vintage

4

Vintage

5

Vintage

PRACTICE YOUR EXERCISES HERE

1920s Serif Script

Serif script is a mixture of vintage script and the serif formation. This style has a very 1920s feel to it and it looks great inside a serif composition. Follow the exercises below to master this script.

1. On the practice pages, connect the first and third sets of dots with a ruler. These new lines will become your ascender and descender guides. Draw out the 65-degree vertical slant guidelines as shown.

2. Start by drawing out the skeleton with a pencil, making sure that the capital letters at the start of the words reach the ascender and descender heights. This gives a balanced aesthetic to the capital letters and allows room for creativity. You can add a flourish for balance as seen in image two.

3. Now start to add weight. Draw the stems with the same thickness and do the same with the bowls, conforming to the 65-degree vertical line.

4. In image 4 the red circles highlight the serif forms, which are either square serifs, for the rectangular letterforms, or circular for the circular letterforms.

5. Using tracing paper or a light box, sketch over your word with a sharp pencil. Keep in mind that the flourishes should be balanced and have the same thin and thick points as the letterforms. Finally, fill in the word with a fine-liner.

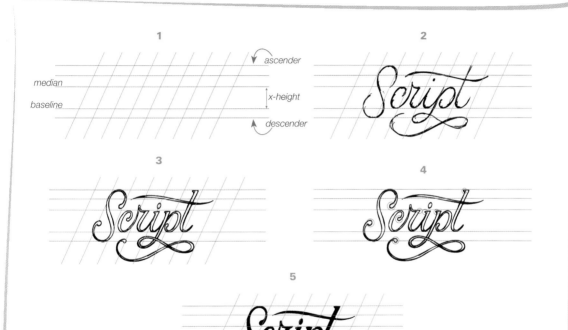

PRACTICE YOUR EXERCISES HERE

Hand Lettered Serif

Serifs are the pointed edges and tips of letterforms. They were created to balance the letters and to keep the alphabet uniform. Serif letterforms originated with the Romans, who used flat brushes and chisels to create type. In this tutorial you'll learn how to create serif letterforms; they are very similar to block lettering and sans serif, the only differences being the serifs and the weight.

1. If you are using your own paper, start by creating two guide lines as shown, you could use the width of a ruler to make drawing the guides easier and more consistent.

2. Lightly draw out the skeleton of the word you want to write in pencil. Keep in mind that the letters should be capitals, also remember to add the serifs so that you space the letters out correctly.

3. Drawing lightly, create weight around the word skeleton.

4. The weight of the letterforms should keep to this pattern: Thick for the vertical lines and thin for the horizontal lines. When you're dealing with a rounded shape such as the "S," the weight change should be drawn in gradually, and not abruptly.

5. Lightly shade in your lines with a pencil and, once you're happy, ink the lines with a fine-liner or thin pen.

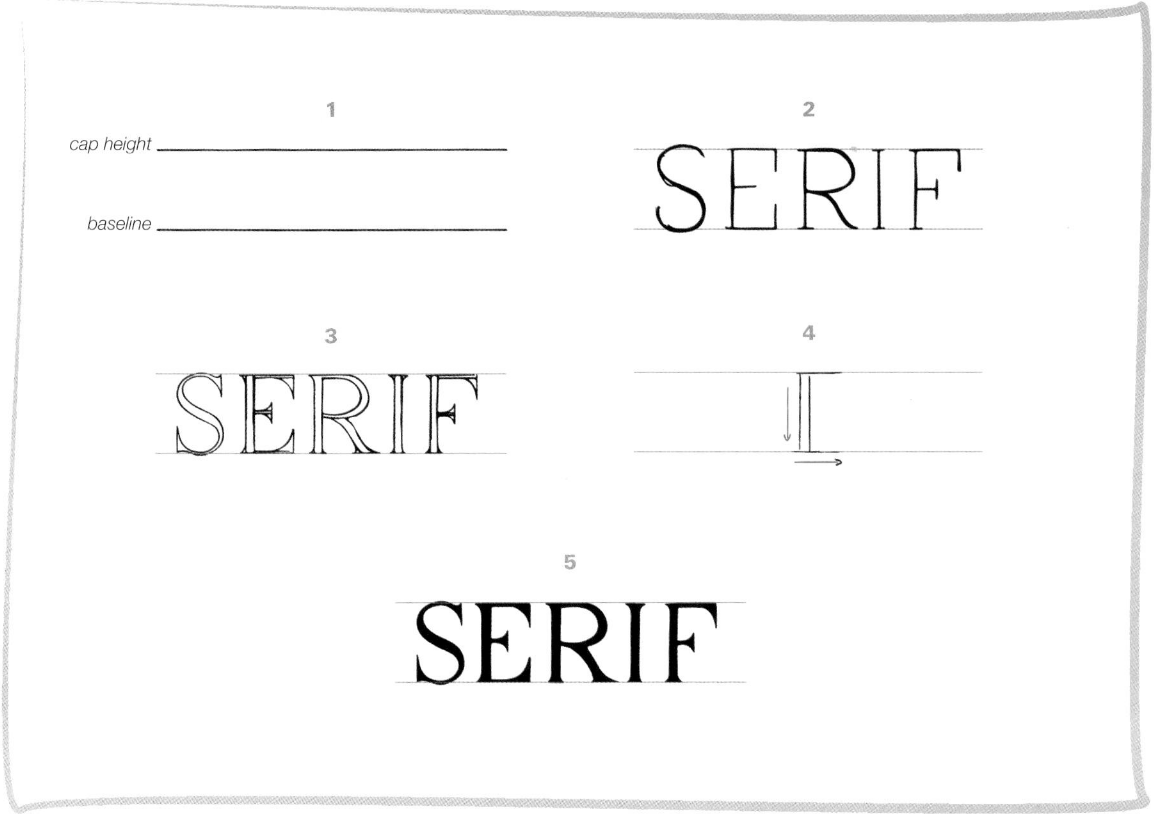

1

cap height _____

baseline _____

2

SERIF

3

SERIF

4

5

SERIF

PRACTICE YOUR EXERCISES HERE

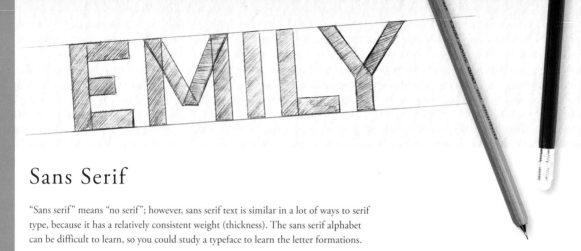

Sans Serif

"Sans serif" means "no serif"; however, sans serif text is similar in a lot of ways to serif type, because it has a relatively consistent weight (thickness). The sans serif alphabet can be difficult to learn, so you could study a typeface to learn the letter formations.

1. If you are using your own paper, draw out your guides as shown. On the following pages, connect the first and fourth sets of dots. These lines will become your guides for ascenders and descenders.

2. Begin by sketching the word's skeleton. The spaces in-between each letterform should be wider than usual because the weight of the letterforms will compensate for it.

3. When you're working with rounded or circular sans serif letterforms they must overshoot the x-height guides as shown in image 3. This also applies to the kerning of the letterforms.

4. Now you can begin to add weight to the letterforms. Each letter should have a consistent weight, for instance the "a," "n," "r," "i," and "f" should have the same thickness horizontally and vertically. You'll start to notice that

each letterform has attributes of other letterforms; for example, the stem of the "a," "n," and "r" look exactly like the "i."

5. Once you've added the weight and you're happy with the letterforms, using tracing paper or a light box, sketch over the letters with a sharp pencil. After this, you can fill the rest in using a fine-liner.

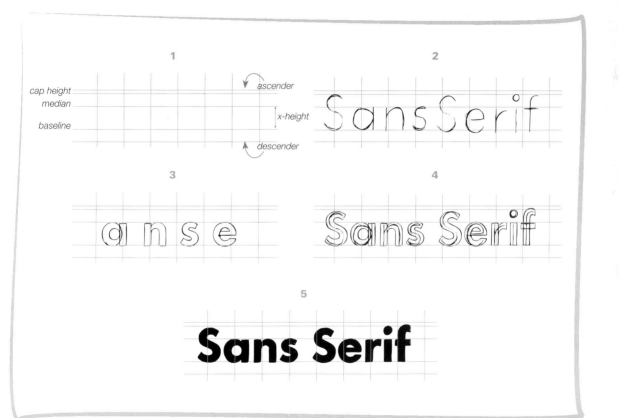

PRACTICE YOUR EXERCISES HERE

Minimal Serif

The most amazing attribute of the serif letterform is that you're able to add and take away elements to create different and unique styles and compositions. In this tutorial you'll learn how to create a minimalist style of serif letterforms.

1. If using your own paper, start by drawing your guides with a ruler. On the practice pages, connect the first and third sets of dots to form your cap height and descender guides.

2. Draw the full skeleton of your lettering with a pencil. Don't be tempted to add or take away any elements of the letterforms just yet, you need to see if the lettering works in its most basic form first.

3. Notice the letter "A" in image 3 overshoots the cap height. This is done purposefully to keep the letterforms optically balanced. The same applies for the letters "V" and "W."

4. Start to add weight to your lettering. It's important to remember to draw out the full letterforms at first as this will help you to make sure that the kerning and balance is optically correct.

5. Using tracing paper or a light box, trace over the letterforms you have drawn; however, this time, miss out all of the thinner lines but keep the serifs. This is the basis of the minimal style of lettering.

6. Now, go ahead and fill in the lettering with a fine-liner. Notice that you can still read the word even though you haven't kept any of the thinner lines!

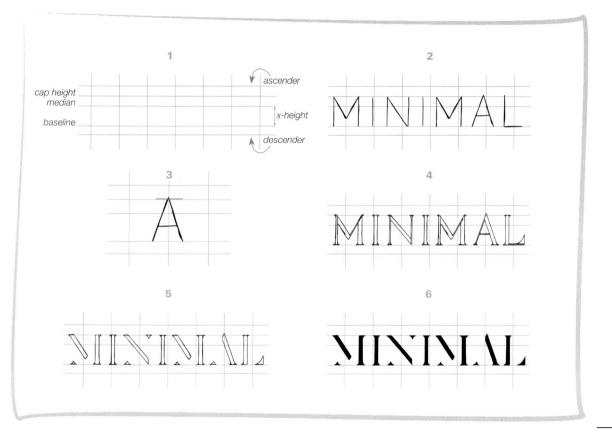

PRACTICE YOUR EXERCISES HERE

Block Serif

Sometimes the differences in weight and thickness of the serif alphabet limits the possibilities for using the typeface in creative applications. In this tutorial you'll learn a unique way to transform the aesthetics of the serif letterform to give it a bolder style.

1. If you are using your own paper, start by drawing your guides with your ruler. For pages 96–97, connect the first and third sets of dots. These will become your cap height and descender guides.

2. Lightly draw out the skeleton of the letterforms in pencil. If you feel comfortable doing so, you could use a ruler to keep all the lines parallel.

3. Keep in mind the spacing between the letterforms. It should be slightly wider than a normal serif alphabet because you'll be making the overall letterform thicker.

4. Now add a consistent weight to the letterforms. Normally with the serif alphabet we vary the weight of each letter based on the letterforms' direction. The difference with this style is that you'll keep the weight thick all the way throughout the letter.

5. Once you've roughly drawn the letterforms, use tracing paper or a light box and, using a sharp pencil, cleanly trace the letters. Remember to use a ruler if you find it difficult to trace freehand. Once you've traced your lettering use a fine-liner pen to outline it and fill it in.

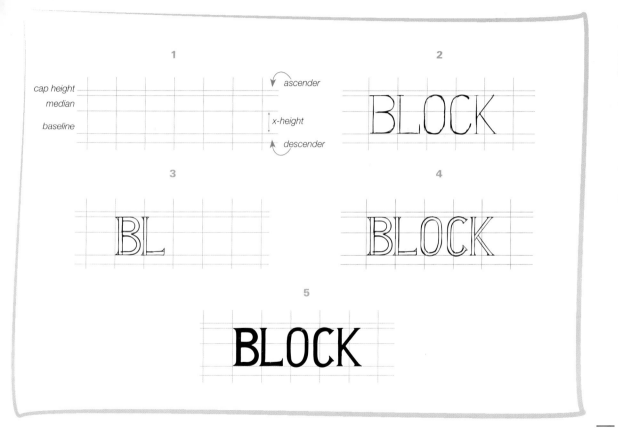

PRACTICE YOUR EXERCISES HERE

Block Lettering

Block lettering is very similar to sans serif lettering. The main difference is the way the lettering is used. Block lettering is also known as "display" type. Display type is normally used on shop windows or in advertisements that need a powerful typeface for a powerful message.

1. If you are using your own paper, start by drawing your guides. If you are using the practice pages, connect the first and fourth sets of dots to create your ascender and descender lines. Make sure you draw the vertical guides as straight as possible. You can do this by using a ruler or a T-square to ensure the angles are correct.

2. Now, using a pencil, draw the skeleton of the lettering as shown in image 2. Make sure you take into account the spacing needed to draw thick, consistent lines inside and outside the shape of the letterform, otherwise your lettering may look too cramped.

3. Image 3 shows the kerning; kerning is the spacing between each letter. Appropriate kerning is essential to making sure your word is legible and balanced. The lines in-between the letters in image 3 show that even though the spacing of the letterforms is metrically different, they are optically the same. Measure your spacing optically, not metrically.

4. Start adding weight to the letterforms, ensuring all lines are of a consistent weight. This can be difficult to judge at first, but with practice you'll start to develop an "eye" for it and be able to easily spot any mistakes you make.

5. Use a fine-liner pen to outline and fill in the lettering. If you need to, use a ruler to keep vertical and horizontal lines perfectly straight.

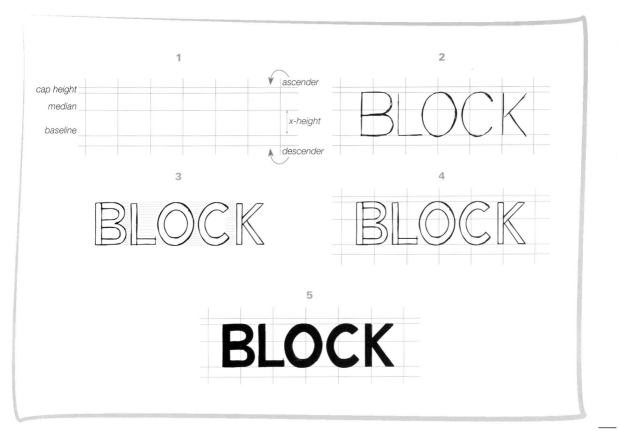

1

cap height
median
baseline

ascender
x-height
descender

2

BLOCK

3

BLOCK

4

BLOCK

5

BLOCK

PRACTICE YOUR EXERCISES HERE

Serif Formations

When using a flat brush—just as when using a brush pen—the thick strokes are created when the brush is performing a downstroke. The thinner lines are created when the brush is maintaining an angle and performing a sidestroke. This tutorial will show you how to create serif formations.

1. Create your guides. Use your ruler and a pencil to join all sets of dots on the following page. The top line on the page will be your ascender guide. Use the rest of the lines to replicate the spacing shown opposite. This doesn't need to be exact. Using a pencil, start by creating one single vertical line. If you prefer, you can use dot grid or square grid paper to do this.

2. Draw a box around your line. Use the vertical line created in step 1 to judge where to start and stop. Make this rectangle as thick as needed.

3. Create the horizontal strokes at the top and bottom of the rectangle. The lines should be three-quarters of the original vertical rectangle. These should be thinner than the vertical lines.

4. On the ends of the horizontal lines, add small vertical lines. These are the serifs for the letter "E."

5. Now connect the serifs to the rest of the letterform as shown. It's important to note that the connection of the serifs should look smooth.

6. Fill in the letterform.

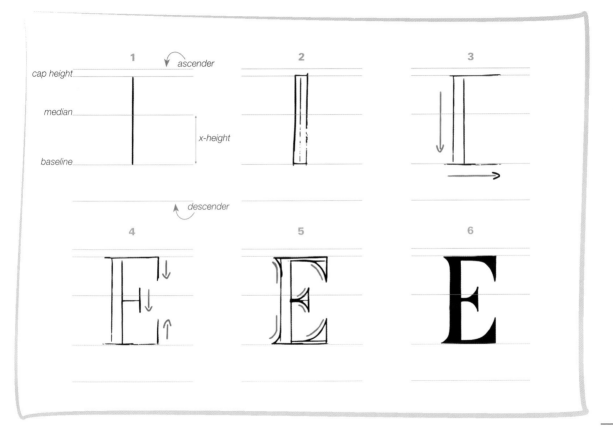

PRACTICE YOUR EXERCISES HERE

Italic Serif

The italic serif letterform adds character and movement to lettering and it also makes for a more interesting composition when using flourishes. In this tutorial you'll learn how to draw these decorative letterforms.

1. If you are using your own paper, start by drawing your guidelines. If you are using the practice pages, connect the first and third sets of dots provided. These will become your cap height and descender lines. You should now draw out the vertical guides at roughly a 70-degree angle.

2. With a pencil, draw the skeleton of the letterforms, making sure that you use a ruler at a 70-degree angle for all vertical lines. The letterforms are italicized by this angle so it is important to make sure that this is consistent.

3. Now start to add weight to the letters, taking care to keep the thick and thin areas consistent all the way through. Keep in mind that all horizontal lines within the word should remain at a 90-degree angle. If you don't do this the lettering will be distorted.

4. Now go ahead and fill in the letterforms with a fine liner. If you're concerned about spoiling the beautiful lines you've made with ink, try using tracing paper or a light box.

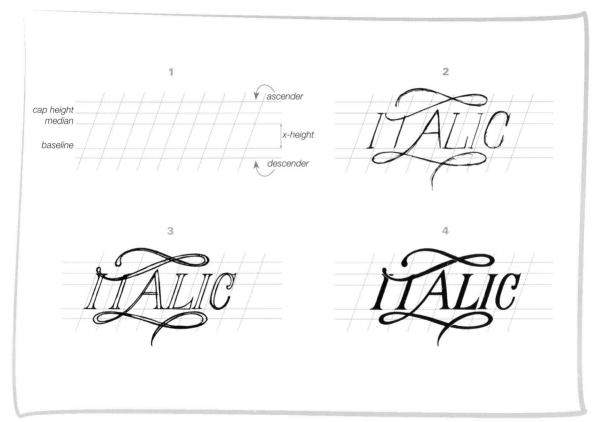

PRACTICE YOUR EXERCISES HERE

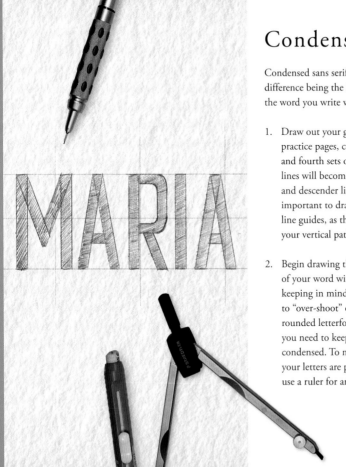

Condensed Sans Serif

Condensed sans serif type is exactly the same as sans serif type. The only difference being the letterforms and spacing are condensed. This means the word you write will have the appearance of being tall and striking.

1. Draw out your guides. On the practice pages, connect the first and fourth sets of dots. These lines will become your ascender and descender lines. It's also important to draw the vertical line guides, as they will establish your vertical path.

2. Begin drawing the skeleton of your word with a pencil, keeping in mind that you need to "over-shoot" on circular and rounded letterforms and that you need to keep the kerning condensed. To make sure that your letters are perfectly vertical, use a ruler for any straight lines.

3. When you're drawing type, you can use the box method as shown in image 3. This involves creating consistent rectangular boxes, which you use to form the letter shape.

4. Now, start to add weight to the letterforms using the box method. Each letterform needs to be consistently sized to a rectangle that can fit around it. Use a ruler to create the straight vertical and horizontal lines to keep it neat.

5. Using tracing paper or a light box, trace over your word using a sharp pencil and a ruler. Once you're happy with the outline, fill in the word with a fine-liner pen.

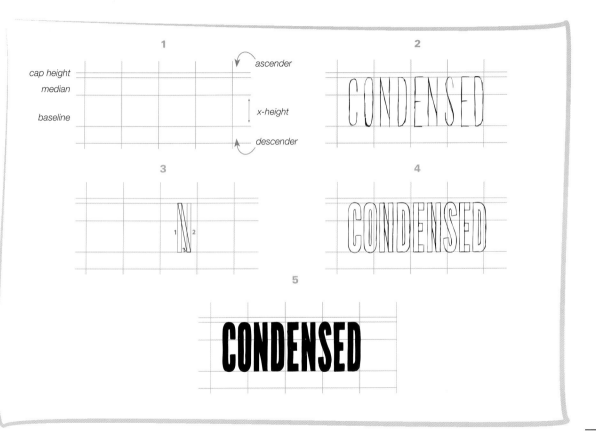

PRACTICE YOUR EXERCISES HERE

Outline Cursive

Outline script adds lightness and character to lettering and is not difficult to do. The main trick with this lettering style is consistency. This tutorial will teach you ways to practice that.

1. When using your own paper, use a ruler to draw out the horizontal guides. On the following pages, connect the first and third sets of dots with a ruler and pencil and use them as your cap height and descender lines. It's important to keep your vertical lines at a 65-degree angle as this is what gives this lettering style a unique flow.

2. Draw the skeleton of the letterforms with a pencil. The main thing to remember with this style of lettering is the flow. Also, make sure all the bowls of the letters are spacious and circular.

3. Start adding weight to the letters, but keep in mind that the connectors of each letter should be very thin, this is what provides the contrast between the thick and thin areas.

4. Notice how the top of the letters are flowing and pointed in image 4. This is an optional extra flourish, which can add a "leafy" and natural flow to the lettering.

5. Now for the tricky part: using tracing paper and a thick black pen trace the outline of the lettering. You may need to try out different pen thicknesses to get the desired effect.

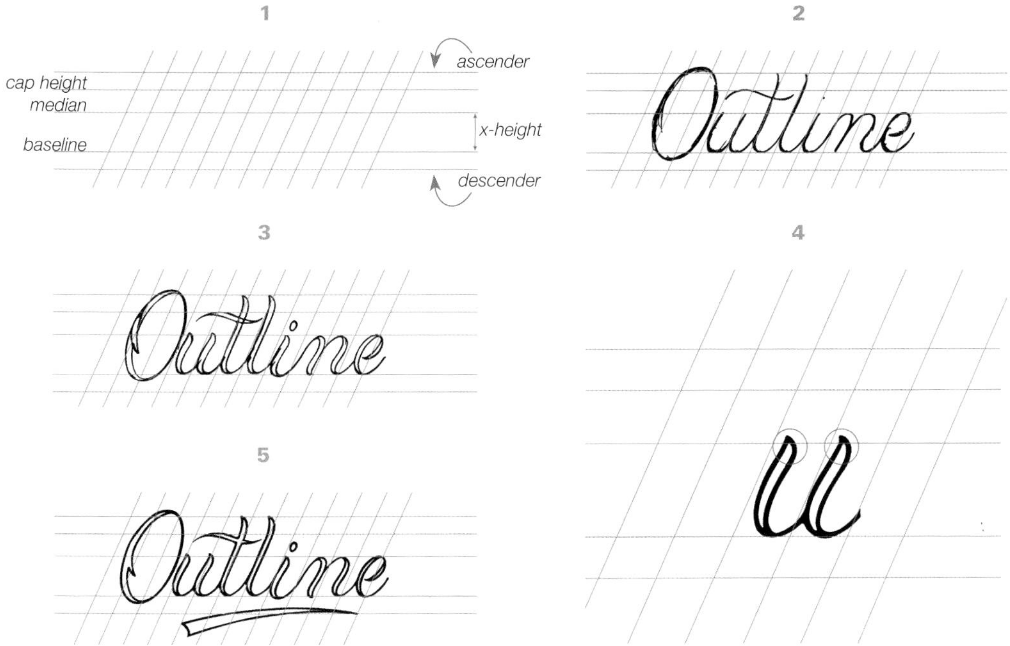
1
2
3
4
5
ascender
cap height
median
x-height
baseline
descender
Outline
Outline
Outline

PRACTICE YOUR EXERCISES HERE

Outline Serif

Serif letterforms are great for adding and taking away different attributes. When drawn correctly they always seem to be legible no matter how you change them! In this tutorial you'll learn how to create an outlined serif word mark. This style is great for highlighting certain words within a hand-lettered composition.

1. When using your own paper, start by creating your guidelines. You could use the width of a ruler to make drawing the guides easier and more consistent. If you are using the pages provided, connect the first set of dots to create your cap height line and use the rest of the lines as desired to create the spacing shown opposite.

2. Now, using a pencil, lightly draw out the skeleton of the word you want to letter. Keep in mind that the letters should be capitalized. Also remember to add lines for the serifs so that you don't run the risk of incorrectly spacing the letterforms.

3. Drawing lightly, as you did for step 2, create weight around the word skeleton.

4. Now for the tricky part: adding the thick outline to the letters. Using some tracing paper or a light box, with a sharp pencil, draw around the letterforms again. Use a ruler if you find it difficult to draw consistently straight lines. Once you're happy, use a thick pen to trace over the outline of the lettering. If you're looking for a rustic/vintage look do this freehand.

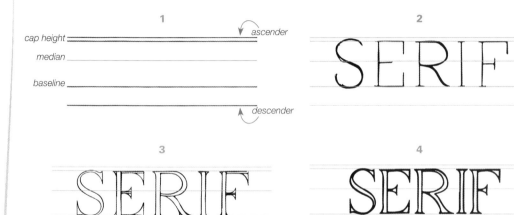

1

cap height ———————————————— ↶ ascender

median ——————————————————

baseline ——————————————————

————————————————— ↰ descender

2

SERIF

3

SERIF

4

SERIF

PRACTICE YOUR EXERCISES HERE

Lettering in a Circle

One of the hardest letter design challenges is mastering drawing your letterforms correctly inside shapes or following shapes. The trick for lettering inside circular shapes is as simple as understanding the rhythm and pattern of the type. Follow the steps below to practice this.

1. Using a compass and pencil, lightly draw out two circles. Don't move the point of your compass, just make the second circle ⅜ in (1 cm) larger or smaller. Now add centered vertical and horizontal guides straight through the middle of the circle.

2. The next step is to use the compass to dot around the edges of the circle at regular intervals. This will give you the guidelines necessary to create your letters.

3. Now use your ruler and draw straight lines from the dots you've just made to the center of the circle. The center is where your compass initially penetrated the paper. These lines help you determine the vertical direction the letterforms should take.

4. Start lightly drawing out your letterforms. The vertical angle of the letters should match up with the guidelines as shown. This is quite a difficult technique to master so it will take practice, but once you've repeated this method a few times it'll become second nature for similar compositions.

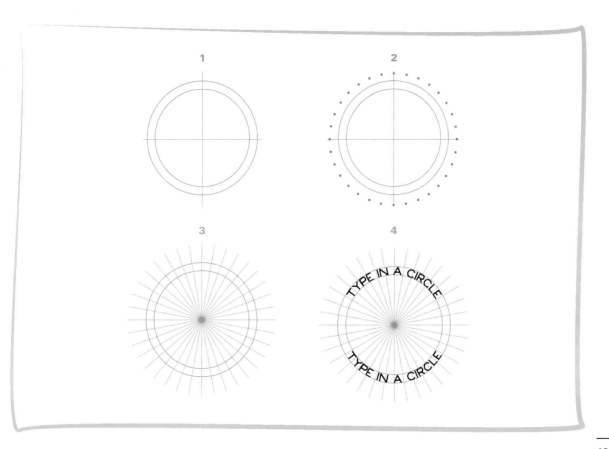

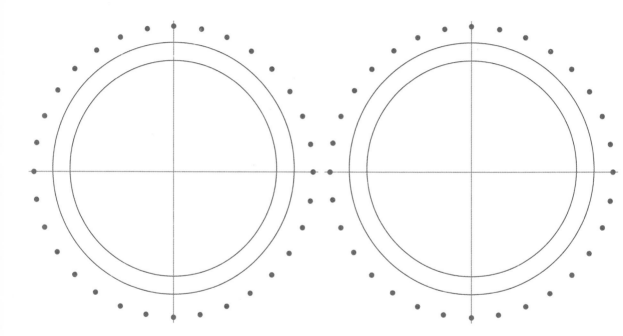

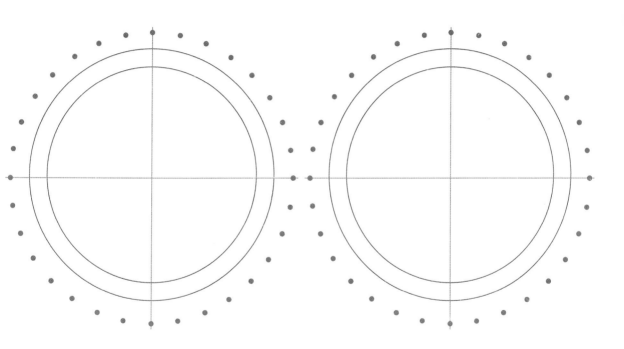

Signature Style

The signature style is one of the quicker styles of hand lettering; it uses a natural cursive form with a fluid arm as the skeleton for the word before weight is added.

1. Use plain or dotted paper and establish the guides: using a ruler draw the cap height, baseline, and median. Usually, the median is three quarters the height of the cap height, meaning the x-height is relatively small compared to the cap height. If you are using the practice pages, connect the first, second, and third sets of dots. These will become your cap height, median, and descender line respectively.

2. Very loosely, using joined-up cursive writing, write your word with a pencil. As you'll see in image 2, it doesn't have to be neat, aim for quick and loose.

3. Add weight to the text: as you did for Vintage Brush Script (see page 74), add a consistent weight to the downstrokes. As you'll see in image 3, this gives a signature style brush weight to the piece. Using tracing paper or a light box, neatly trace over the lines with a sharp pencil—this will clean up the lines and make any mistakes more noticeable so that they can be fixed.

4. Now, using a fine-liner or a .05 Micron, outline over the traced pencil lines and then fill in the work. Keep in mind that this style is meant to look rustic not perfect, you don't have to stick to the guidelines all the time, be creative and find a signature style that suits you.

1

cap height ——————————————— ↓ *ascender*

median ————————————————
baseline ———————————————— *x-height*

—————————————— ↑ *descender*

2

Signature

3

Signature

4

Signature

PRACTICE YOUR EXERCISES HERE

Bowl Cursive

Bowl Cursive is traditionally created using an italic fountain pen or a chisel-tip brush. The main feature of this style is the thickness in the "bowl" of the letter. In image 4, you'll see that the thickness lies at the bowl (bottom) of the letter giving the piece a traditional 1920s-style feel.

1. Begin by drawing out standard type guides on your paper. Then add 65-degree vertical type guides over the first guides—these indicate the cursive slant for the work.

2. Now draw the skeleton in lightly with a pencil, keeping to the guides you've drawn. If you're not sure what to write, just copy the word used here.

3. In image 3, you'll see the bowls of the letters conforming to a perfect circle (as much as possible) in the skeleton. Keeping the bowls consistent unites the work, making it flow. Good typography is all about consistency.

4. It's now time to add some weight to the letterforms. Remember to keep the bowls thicker and the lines going up to the next letter thinner throughout the whole word, as shown in image 4.

5. Next, using tracing paper or a light box, trace the word using a sharp pencil, then go over it with a .05 Micron. Finally, fill in the word.

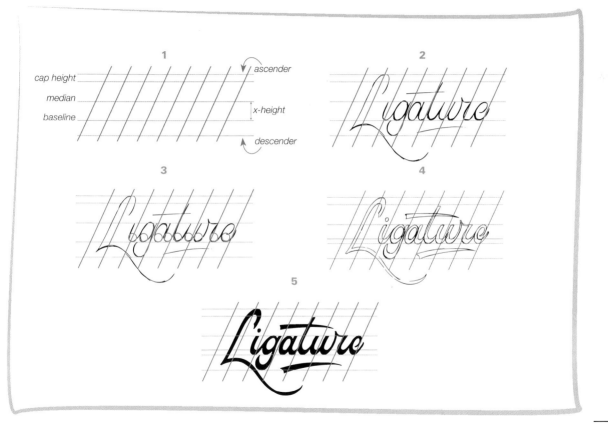

1

cap height
median
baseline
ascender
x-height
descender

2

3

4

5

PRACTICE YOUR EXERCISES HERE

Gallery

BELOW This retro style composition makes use of banners, non-lettering elements, and curved guides.

BLESSED ARE ✝ THE PEACE-MAKERS

Dream

COME HOME

DREAM BIG

Whiskey Lettering

ABOVE The key to great hand lettering is practice. It's a good idea to take your sketchbook and a pencil everywhere you go so that you can record inspiring type when you're out and about.

LEFT An oblique pen holder with nib and ink were used to write this stylish thank you message. Drawn decorative elements are used to balance the composition.

15 Variations and Extras

Layout for Lettering

Lettering and calligraphy can look great even if it's just one word. But when you're trying to letter a quote or a favorite lyric, it's important to plan ahead to create an interesting composition. Here you will learn about thumbnails; simple shapes, such as squares or circular arches, which are used to establish a guide for lettering designs.

1. For this exercise squared or dotted paper can be helpful. Draw a rectangle of any size in similar proportions to an A4 sheet of paper—this will be the basis of your thumbnail.

2. Start adding in shapes, for arches or rectangles, but bear in mind that these shapes are guides into which you will fit your calligraphy or lettering, so keep the spacing correct!

3. Add arches to guide the shapes of the key words. This will create emphasis and substance in the finished design.

4. Try and keep the shapes simple. Here, a simple line has been added to create contrast between the less important words and the key words.

5. Only add a few interesting guides to the shapes and keep the amount of guides to the amount of words that you can fit.

6. Here, another simple, straight guide was added to give balance and symmetry throughout the design. You can experiment with this technique, interspersing more complex shapes with simpler ones.

7. Add shading to the guides to gain a better visual idea of the negative space.

8. Image 8 shows more basic examples of lettering composition. The trick is to make the shapes look clear and balanced so that your letterforms are legible and balanced.

PRACTICE YOUR EXERCISES HERE

Inline Lettering

In calligraphy and lettering, the simplest of tweaks can give rise to the most substantial of impacts, so it's important to be diligent and follow the steps correctly to achieve the desired effect. This lesson looks at inline lettering, which is great for conveying a particularly "retro" style.

1. First, draw the skeleton of your word on squared or dotted paper with a pencil. You can also use a ruler to keep everything in line if you prefer.

2. Just as you did for Block Lettering (see page 98), lightly draw out the rest of the word's structure. Remember to keep your lines as straight as possible.

3. Now you can thicken the lines. Make sure you keep everything even or the final product could appear bumpy. Using a thick marker pen might help—the wider nib means you may need just one stroke to cover the length of the letter.

4. Draw a straight line down the center of your letters with a thinner marker pen. If you're struggling to keep your lines straight, use a ruler to guide you. In time, and with practice you will learn to draw straight lines without a ruler.

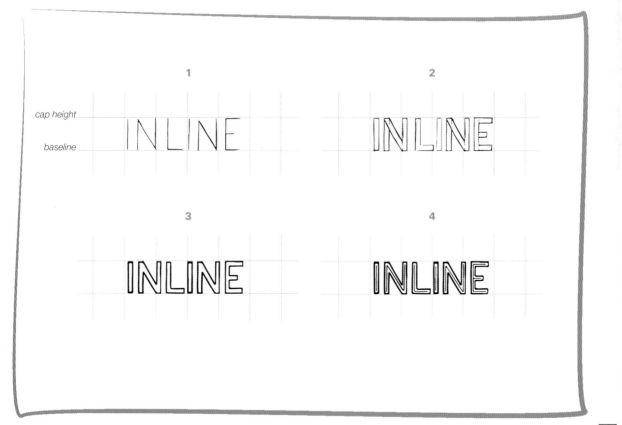

PRACTICE YOUR EXERCISES HERE

Collaborating with the Brush Pen

Adding a textured effect to hand lettering using a brush pen can produce striking and natural-looking designs; achieving a dynamic that seamlessly blends together different styles.

It is a good idea to decide on the word or phrase you want to brush pen before you start your design. This will give you a chance to practice your brush strokes on a separate piece of paper—it will also reinforce the muscle memory needed to beautifully replicate your chosen words in the final design.

Learning to use the brush pen effectively only comes with practice, but once you are confident, you can use this technique to give your designs an edge that really showcases the breadth of your skills. You could revisit section 1 for the tutorial on Brush Lettering, page 30, if you want more practice.

1. Sketch out your drawn lettering and the skeleton of your word using your normal marker or pencil.

2. Once you are happy with the spacing of your design, finish off the drawn lettered words.

3. Now you can pick up your brush pen and add flesh to the skeleton of your chosen word.

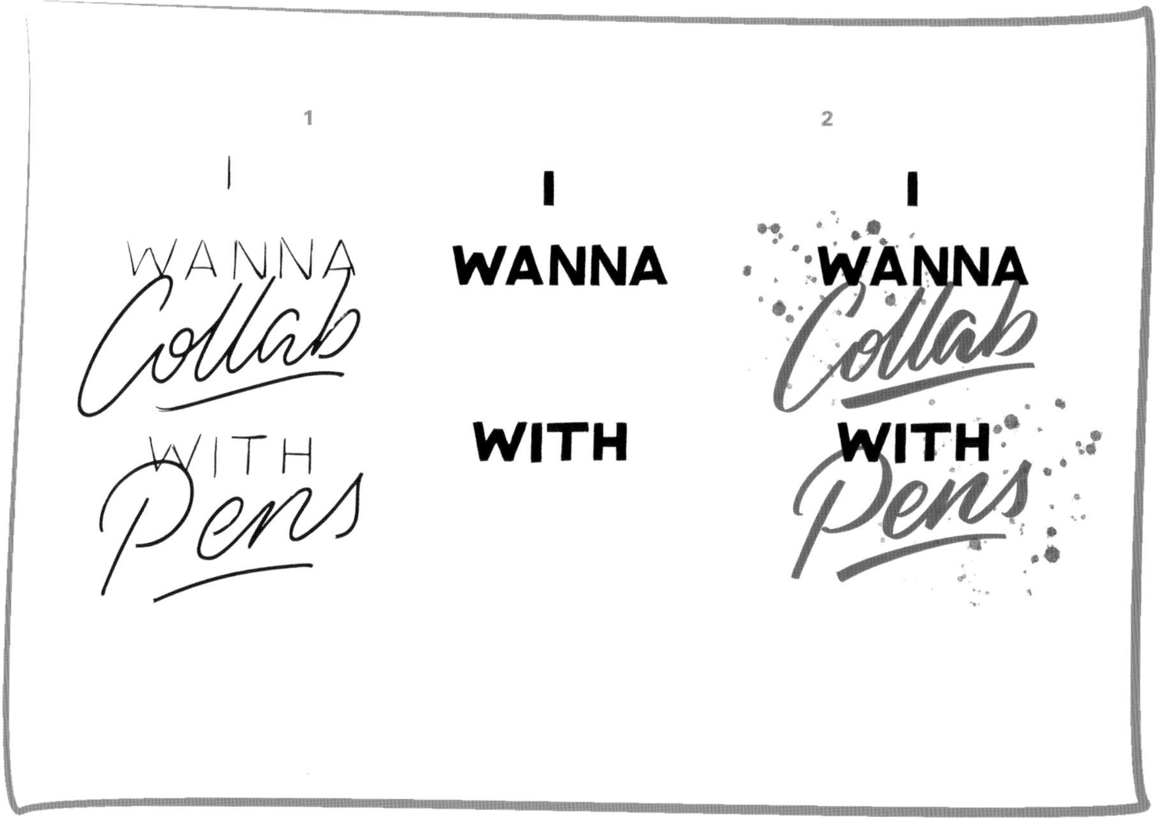
1
I
WANNA
Collab
WITH
Pens
I
WANNA
WITH
2
I
WANNA
Collab
WITH
Pens

PRACTICE YOUR EXERCISES HERE

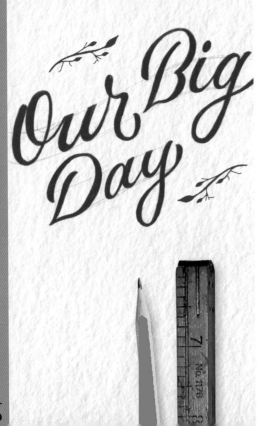

Composition Guides

Guides are essential when it comes to calligraphy and hand lettering; they help you to retain consistency and straight lines while you're working, and are the foundation of good calligraphy.

1. Using a ruler, draw one straight line. Try to keep the line parallel to the paper you're working on.

2. Keep your ruler in place and draw a second line using the bottom half of your ruler. This ensures that the lines you've drawn are parallel to one another.

3. Now turn your ruler so that it's vertical. The vertical lines you draw now will help you to remain consistent when creating vertical lines for lettering or calligraphy.

4. Now try to recreate the S-curve in image 4. This is drawn freehand, so you don't need to use a ruler. This is an "S-curve guide" and it will enable you to easily draw out your letterforms in a creative and flowing way.

5. Now draw two S-curve guides, parallel to one another.

6. Depending on what angle your letterforms will be following, draw guides for them. In this case, vertical guides were used because the planned lettering will be vertical.

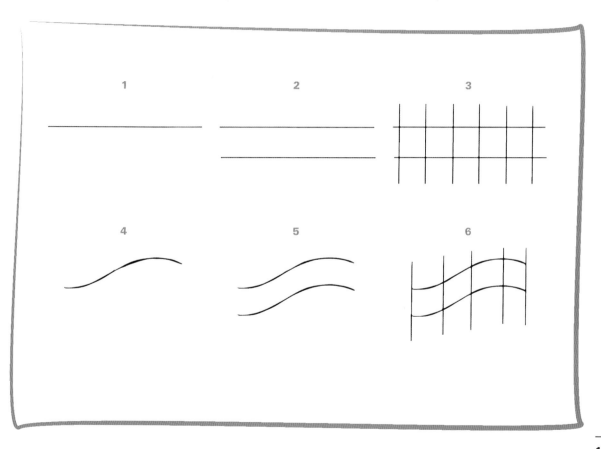

1

2

3

4

5

6

PRACTICE YOUR EXERCISES HERE

Amazing Elements

Lettering and calligraphy are definitely worth the time it takes. Designers have a set font list they can use and certain elements they can afford. Lettering artists can take inspiration from anything and use that in their compositions. Here, you'll learn a process for balancing your lettering composition with non-letter decorative elements.

1. Start by drawing out your lettering. This could be brush, serif, or sans serif. Here, serif lettering in the shape of a flag has been used.

2. Because "Element" is the primary word to be highlighted, it was lettered out first, followed by the less important word, "Amazing." So the first non-letter element incorporated into the design is the banner. The banner is balanced with the design because it flows with the shape of "Element."

3. In image 2, there is a lot of negative space (blank space) in the bottom right. In image 3, this problem is resolved by adding decorative line elements to fill up that space.

Again, these lines conform to the shape of "Element."

4. In image 4, some vintage rustic-style branches and leaves are added to fill in some more space.

5. In image 5, a feeling of movement is added by drawing lines to the outside of the image. This gives the composition more balance and draws the eye to the center.

6. Image 6 shows lines added to complete the rectangular shape of the composition. This also fills in some of the negative space. However, remember that you don't have to fill the negative space!

1

2

3

4

5

6

PRACTICE YOUR EXERCISES HERE

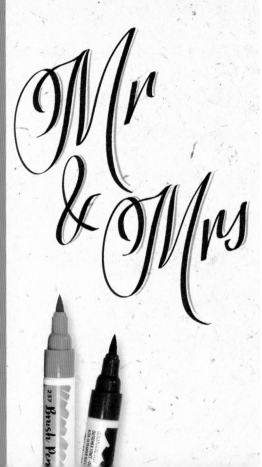

Adding Shadows

Sometimes you want to add a little extra "something" to your lettering; especially if the words are all the same color. So in this tutorial, you'll learn how to add shadows to your lettering work to give it more depth and interest.

1. First, write out a word of your choice. Depending on what kind of shadow you want to create, you can either draft out your letterforms with a pencil or use a brush pen. The brush pen is always easier for this effect as the shadows are more forgiving.

2. When adding shadows to lettering it's important that you keep the shadow at a constant angle. In this case the shadow angle is 320 degrees, which means the light source is at the top left of the lettering. With your brush pen, repeat the lettering at this angle to create the shadow. In image 2 you can see that a pink shadow has been added—note how consistent this is with the basic lettering. You can use any colors you wish for shadows, but different colors have different effects and outcomes, so try different options. Gray shadows for black lettering are always effective.

1

2

PRACTICE YOUR EXERCISES HERE

Creating Depth

Sometimes lettering can appear flat. Here, you'll learn how to remedy that by creating depth in your brush calligraphy or cursive monoline lettering. However, it's worth noting that this technique will only be effective when created with a color saturated brush pen or with watercolor lettering.

1. Start by using either your color brush pen, or a color marker for monoline lettering. Draw out your lettering as you usually would.

2. Wait for your lettering to dry so that it doesn't smudge and, working lightly in pencil, sketch out where the shadows should be. The shadows should appear where one pen or brush stroke crosses another and be determined by the order in which the letters were created. When filling in the shadows, start from the darkest area, as shown in image 2. Shade in the shadows with your pencil, gradually lightening the pressure as you work away from the deepest shadows to achieve the right effect.

NOTE:
When you're shading the darkest areas, make sure you don't use the pointed end of your pencil. Your pencil should be as flat as you can possibly get it to the paper while still maintaining control.

1

Depth

2

Depth

PRACTICE YOUR EXERCISES HERE

Brush Flourishing

Flourishing is a technique that is seen throughout pointed pen calligraphy, but which is not frequently seen in brush calligraphy. Here, you'll discover some of the ways you can easily add flourishes to your letterforms to bring the words to life!

1. Image 1 shows two examples of a lowercase "h." The first letter has a conventional stem and the second has a flourish. Using a brush pen, try to recreate the flourish in one movement of the pen, as indicated by the arrows.

2. Image 2 shows a lowercase "g" with flourishing added to the descender. Recreate this, starting from the asterisk and following the arrows. Look carefully at the image to get a sense of the weight of each segment.

3. Image 3 shows two variations of an uppercase "R." Again, the flourishing is added to the descender height. To recreate the flourished letter follow the arrows in Image 3.

4. In image 4, you'll see the word "name." Because there aren't many opportunities to add flourishes without affecting the legibility, just the bottom of the word is flourished with a swash—a quick stroke, applied with hard pressure that is gradually released.

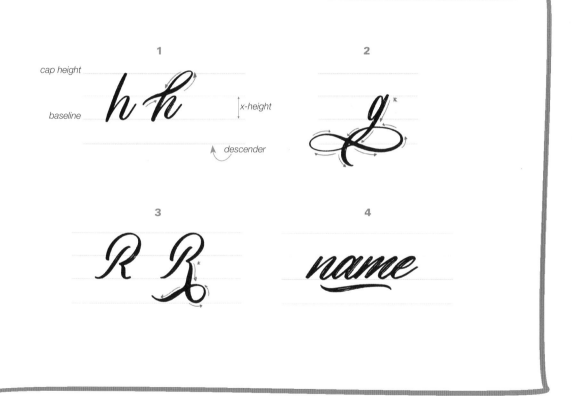

1

cap height

baseline

x-height

descender

2

3

4

name

5. Image 5 shows a standard figure of 8 flourish, which is used to embellish a lot of calligraphy work. To create the smooth lines, start from the red asterisk, and then move to the right and left. This kind of flourish has to be practiced many times in order for your muscle memory to develop.

6. The key to flourishing is to maintain space and balance within your lettering. Image 6 shows brush lettering with two flourishes: The "F" flourish provides balance and space to the word; and the second flourish—a swash at the bottom— is an aesthetic flourish.

5

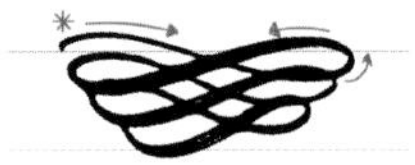

6

PRACTICE YOUR EXERCISES HERE

Serif and Brush Lettering

Serif and brush lettering is highly versatile and attractive; there are many different possible variations available, including the sans serif option shown above. In this exercise you'll learn how to superimpose brush lettering onto serif or vice versa.

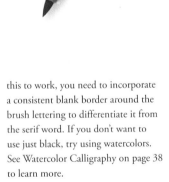

1. Decide which two words you would like to letter out. Here, "Brush" and "SERIF" are used. Draw out the second word first, in the serif typeface. This doesn't have to be perfect because you will use tracing paper or a light box to produce the final composition.

2. Using a light box or tracing paper, draw out your brush lettering over the serif lettering. Make sure the brush lettering is balanced and is at the right size to fill the serif lettering.

3. Once you have completed the brush lettering, using a pencil, trace out the serif letters as seen in the image. For this to work, you need to incorporate a consistent blank border around the brush lettering to differentiate it from the serif word. If you don't want to use just black, try using watercolors. See Watercolor Calligraphy on page 38 to learn more.

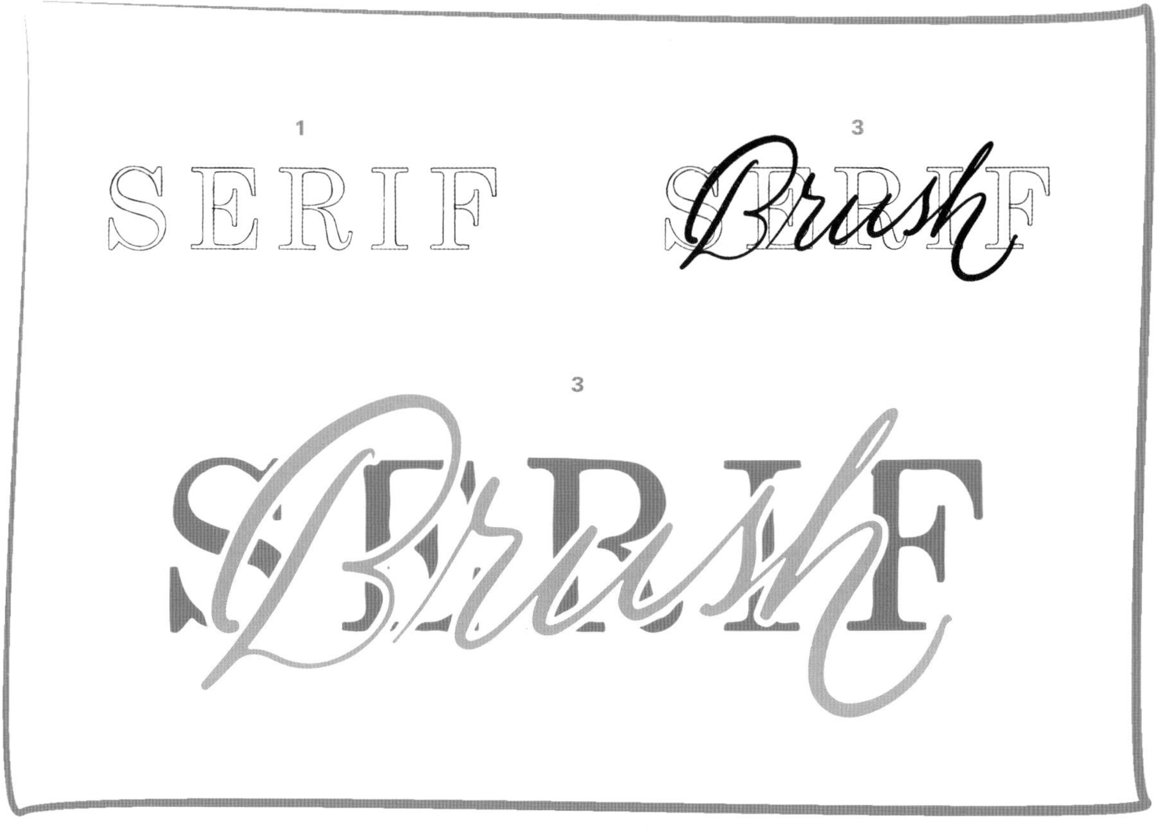

1
SERIF
3
Brush
SERIF
3
Brush
SERIF

PRACTICE YOUR EXERCISES HERE

Serif Flourishing

Flourishing is the art of embellishing type, it brings balance and an elegance to calligraphy and hand lettering. In this lesson, you'll be given an example of how you can flourish your serif lettering.

1. Start by drawing out the skeleton of your lettering. Make sure to leave enough space in-between each letter for when you add weight.

2. Using tracing paper, go over the lettering, but this time flourish and embellish certain parts of the word. Make sure that when you do this you retain the balance and legibility of the word.

3. Once you have established the flourished skeleton, add weight to the letterforms as shown in the Hand Lettered Serif exercise on page 82.

4. Using another sheet of tracing paper outline the lettering with a fine-liner or a Micron .05 pen. Then use a thicker, 8mm fine-liner to fill in the lettering.

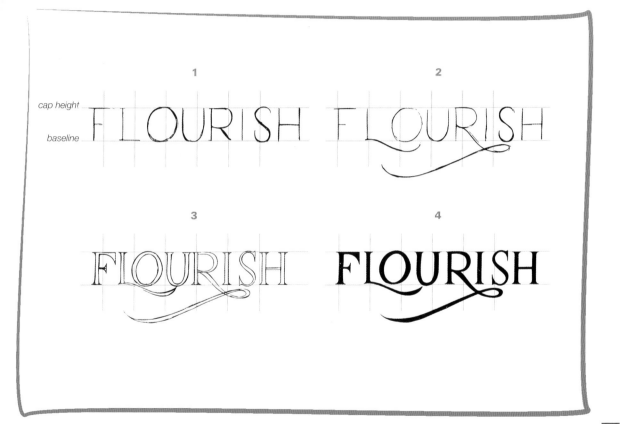

PRACTICE YOUR EXERCISES HERE

Using Banners

Banners and flags are a way to break up the layout and composition of your lettering. They can be used to highlight key words and they're great for adding symmetry.

1. To start drawing a two-part banner, create two S-curved rectangles. Make sure the first rectangle shows above the second—this will give a three-dimensional effect.

2. Next, draw the banners on either side. The top of the side banners should appear to be beneath the banners drawn in step 1.

3. Once you have a flat image of the banners, start to create the folds. Draw the folds lightly at first because it's easy to make mistakes with the angles and perspective.

4. You should now have the basis of your final banner. Go over this with a fine liner or increase the weight of the lines by tracing over them with a thick marker pen.

5. Using the curvature of the banner as a guide, add your lettering to the center of the banner.

PRACTICE YOUR EXERCISES HERE

Vintage Effect

If you look at old sign lettering, you'll see how beautifully aged the type looks. The vintage effect might seem difficult to achieve but in reality there are only a few techniques needed to give your lettering this look.

1. Use a black ink brush pen, or draw out your lettering as shown in image 1. As you can see, image 1 looks like normal brush calligraphy. This will form the basis of the vintage effect. It doesn't really matter what style of lettering you use, but brush lettering will enable you to get the most out of this effect.

2. Image 2 shows the type with the vintage effect applied to it. The difference between image 1 and 2 is that there are no sharp edges in image 2.

3. Image 3 is a close-up example, highlighting the sharp edges before the effect has been applied. Sharp edges give the letterforms more of a modern look, so the goal is to make these edges rounder.

4. When you have lettered out your word, using the same pen, roughly round out all sharp corners. It's important to use the same or similar ink to the original pen, otherwise you run the risk of having different shades of the same color.

1

Old Vintage

2

Old Vintage

3

Old

4

Old

PRACTICE YOUR EXERCISES HERE

Watercolor Inking

When drawing out lettering, sometimes the choice of inks you have available to fill in the letters can be uninspiring and not as vibrant as you would really like. This is where watercolor comes into play. Watercolor is great for filling in lettering, it can be used to brilliant effect it to produce a vintage look and it's also much quicker to fill with than fine-liner or marker pens.

1. First, draw out your lettering lightly with a pencil. You can draw any style of lettering that you like—sans serif, serif, brush, or a combination of them all in a composition. Once you've drawn out your lettering, make sure that you don't fill any of it with ink! Watercolor is a delicate paint, so if you use any other ink on your composition it will show through and you won't achieve the desired effect.

2. Once you're happy with your drawn lettering, using a round or pointed watercolor brush, load your brush with watercolor, taking care to ensure that the paint isn't too thick as there should be a "loose" feeling to the painting. Once you're happy with the mixture of paint and water, start to fill in the lettering. The great thing about using watercolors is that you don't need to be too accurate because watercolor has a great finish. Once you've finished filling the lettering, tape the paper to your table (to avoid warping) and let it dry.

1

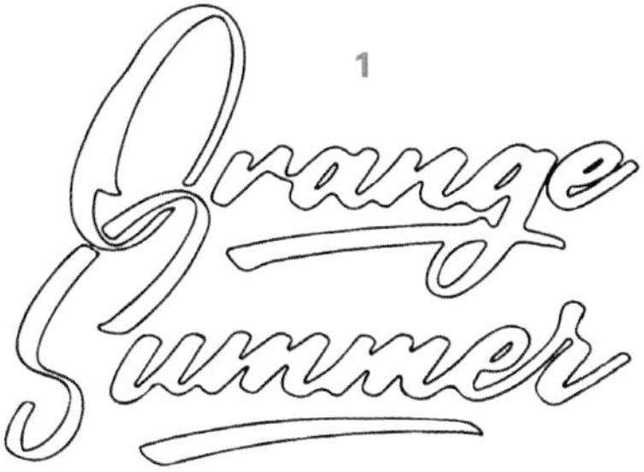

2

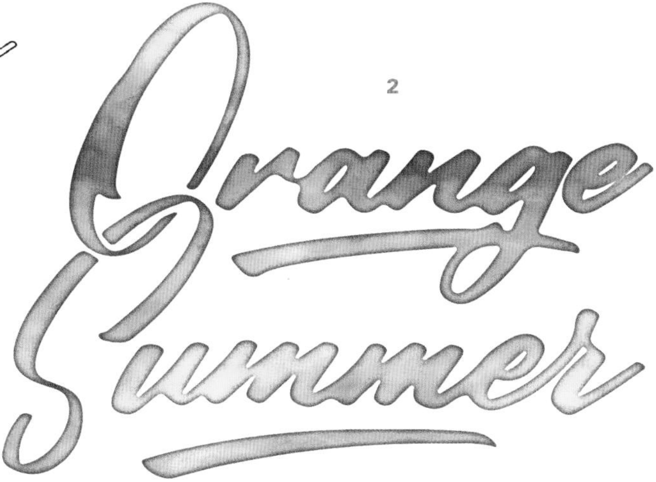

PRACTICE YOUR EXERCISES HERE

Stippling

The stamp effect is known and loved by many lettering artists. It can give a worn and rustic feeling to your lettering, but in many cases, this effect is only being made via computer programs. In this exercise, you'll learn how you can create this effect by hand stippling.

1. Stippling is the art of using very small dots to create texture. Start by using a fine-liner, such as a Micron .05 to create a series of random dots in the shape of a rectangle.

2. Now stipple some more random dots in the middle of the square, the dots should be randomly but evenly placed.

Keep in mind that stippling is a quick technique, so don't feel like you have to be slow!

3. On the right side of the square, start to add another layer of dots. This is going to give a shaded texture. The right side should be darker than the left.

4. Image 4 shows finished lettering where stippling has been applied. When you're lettering, instead of filling in your work with a black fine liner, stipple it so that the middle of each letterform is textured.

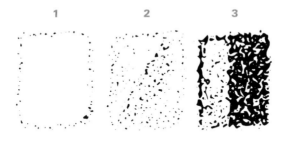

1   2   3

4

Stipple

PRACTICE YOUR EXERCISES HERE